MW00399392

LONG AGO AND FAR AWAY

and Other Short Plays

BY DAVID IVES

★

DRAMATISTS
PLAY SERVICE
INC.

2

LONG AGO
AND FAR AWAY

and Other Short Plays

TABLE OF CONTENTS

LONG AGO AND FAR AWAY

A Winter's Tale

this play is for Lisa Schwarzbaum

Nessun maggior dolore
che ricordarsi del tempo felice
ne la miseria; e ciò sa 'l tuo dottore

Ma s'a conoscer la prima radice
del nostro amor tu hai cotanto affetto,
dirò come colui che piange e dice...

— *Inferno*, Canto V

LONG AGO AND FAR AWAY was produced by Ensemble Studio Theatre (Curt Dempster, Artistic Director), in New York City, in May, 1993. It was directed by Christopher A. Smith; the set design was by H. Peet Foster; the costume design was by Julie Doyle; the lighting design was by Greg MacPherson and the stage manager was Judith Sostek. The cast was as follows:

LAURA .... Crista Moore
GUS .... John Ottavino
JACK .... Baxter Harris
LANDLADY.. Gretchen Walther

CHARACTERS

LAURA, 30

GUS, 30

JACK, 60

LANDLADY

SETTING

The main room of an apartment in New York City. Except for a few boxes at center and a CD player against the wall at right, the place is empty. There is a fireplace at right without a fire in it. A door to the outside up left and an open doorway to a hallway at center.

LONG AGO
AND FAR AWAY

Laura is sitting on a packing box and looking at a pen which she holds in her hand, turning it over and over. After a moment, Gus enters from center carrying a box.

GUS.   This is the end of it. Nine pounds of ancient correspondence. *(Laura says nothing.)* Aloha.
LAURA.   I'm sorry.
GUS.   Lost in space?
LAURA.   Yeah, I was, a little.
GUS.   You're probably exhausted.
LAURA.   No, I'm good. I'm *very* good.
GUS.   Good. Excellent. *(Kisses her.)* Happy day, happy day, happy day. And this is just the prequel. *(He notices an old record album lying on a crate near Laura.)* What's this?
LAURA.   I don't know. I found it when I was cleaning up.
GUS.   "Long Ago and Far Away and Other Great Songs." Looks ancient. *(Holds it to his ear. Timex commercial.)* "But it's *still ticking!*" — Yours?
LAURA.   No, I've never seen it before.
GUS.   A mysterious object. Did you see us in the *Times* today?
LAURA.   We were in the *Times?*
GUS.   *(Reading from newspaper.)* "West 90s apartment near Central Park. Brownstone building. One bedroom, small study, remodeled kitchen, marble fireplace." Of course, they didn't mention that the fireplace doesn't w*ork,* but ...
LAURA.   How do you know it was us?
GUS.   Well. West 90s. Near Park. Fireplace. Sounded like us. And a million other apartments, it's true. But somehow I had

11

this weird feeling they were talking about us.

LAURA.   A woman disappeared.

GUS.   A woman what...?

LAURA.   Did you see that in the paper? A woman in our neighborhood disappeared.

GUS.   New neighborhood or old neighborhood?

LAURA.   This neighborhood.

GUS.   Anybody we know? We'll take her off the Rolodex.

LAURA.   Ruth somebody.

GUS.   Ah. Ruth Somebody. *Her.*

LAURA.   Her husband came home and pots were cooking on the stove — the TV was on — all her clothes were still in the closet — and she was gone.

GUS.   Another reason to move. Can't live in a neighborhood where you have people just *disappearing* on you. I mean what is this? Argentina?

LAURA.   "Vanished without a trace..."

GUS.   She probably ran off with a Hindu ski instructor. Maybe she got caught in a time warp, or an alternative reality. Anyway, she'll be back. Even in a separate reality you need a change of socks.

LAURA.   A couple of years from now we'll probably see her picture in the paper and they'll say she's never been heard from.

GUS.   Mmm. Husband heartbroken. Friends and neighbors baffled. "Ruth was always such a *wonderful* person."

LAURA.   She has to be somewhere. Even if you disappear you don't just ... disappear.

GUS.   You're in a pretty spooky mood tonight. *(Holds up a bottle of wine.)* Care for a final celebratory glass of wine at the old homestead?

LAURA.   Sure.

GUS.   Mmm. Not the most convincing reading of that line I've ever heard.

LAURA.   Yes, please. I'd love some wine.

GUS.   Brilliant. *(Kisses her.)* Are you sure you're okay?

LAURA.   Yeah. Fine.

GUS.   *(Pouring wine.)* Did these people say when they were coming over? The phantom apartment-seekers?

LAURA. No, just tonight sometime.

GUS. I don't see why we have to hang around for them. I told Tony and Bea we'd go out and celebrate. The really meaningful question for tonight being, do we go to the Empire Pagoda for their incomparable cold sesame noodles, to the Empire Dragon for the superb eggplant with garlic sauce, or to the Empire Valley for the killer moo shoo pork. Someplace conducive to dissecting this latest spate of bad movies — including that Lithuanian ode to ennui they sent us to. You're absolutely sure you're all right?

LAURA. I'm splendid.

GUS. I've always said so. *(Hands her a glass of wine.)* Cheers, babe. To better days.

LAURA. Why "*better* days?"

GUS. Well. The new apartment. The great future out there ahead of us. The fact that I got insulted in the street today. Days have got to get better than that.

LAURA. You got insulted...?

GUS. *Still* more reasons to move.

LAURA. On our street?

GUS. Today. And I don't even.... Maybe this was a metaphysical experience. Maybe I hallucinated it. Who knows. Anyway I'm coming up the street and up ahead of me I see this couple sitting on a doorstep about halfway down the block. A man and a woman.

LAURA. Homeless people?

GUS. Just ordinary everyday-looking people. Ergo, probably homeless. Anyway, the guy looks over and sees me coming and he nudges the woman and she looks over at me, so all the time I'm walking by them I can feel them *looking* at me. You know? All this while still saying nothing. So I sail on and I'm probably about two feet past them when I hear the guy turn to the woman — obviously talking about me — and he says to her: *(Significant pause. With a smirk.) "See what I mean?"*

LAURA. "See what I...?"

GUS. "See what I mean?" What the hell is *that* supposed to mean? I never see these people before in my life, then I go walking by and — "See what I mean?" They had to be talking about me. And if I'm the punch line to somebody's story, I'd kind of like to know what the joke is! Is that insulting or what? And most insulting because I don't even know what it means! Any wisdom? Speculation? Thoughts?

LAURA.   Do you know what I think I've just realized?

GUS.   You were the woman on the doorstep? No. Tell me.

LAURA.   I think I've only just realized that this is reality.

GUS.   Excuse me? Did you just say "this is reality"?

LAURA.   I think I've only just realized that I exist.

GUS.   You mean, tonight, or...?

LAURA.   No, I mean.... Lately so often it's like there are these ... moments of illumination ...

GUS.   Mmmmmmmmmmmm.

LAURA.   ... when just for a second or two I realize, I mean I *really* realize, that this — all this — is really here. That it exists. And that I'm part of it. I don't know. Somehow it just recently hit me that when philosophers talk about the nature of reality, they're not talking about words, or ideas, they're talking about things like this box, and this newspaper, and this pen in my hand. Which are all real.

GUS.   Uh-huh.

LAURA.   I am *in* the universe. It's so strange. There's this large empty hole a billion years old and a trillion light years across, and I'm standing on a tiny piece of a small rock flying through it. We are. Everybody is. Right now. At this instant. I exist, and this pen exists. It's sitting in my hand. In my living hand ...

GUS.   Uh-huh. Listen, just click the heels of your ruby slippers together and say "There's no place like home, there's no place like home ..."

LAURA.   Oh go to hell.

GUS.   Go to hell? Come on, Laura. "This is reality" — ?! This is New York. This is hell. This Is Your Life With Ralph Edwards, maybe. But — "this is *reality?*" "I am in the universe?" Okay. I'm sorry. I didn't mean to not take you seriously.

LAURA.   Nice job, buddy.

GUS.   It's just — When somebody says "This is reality," anything you say in response is bound to sound a little trite. What *is* the proper riposte to "This is reality"?

LAURA.   Why does everything have to be a riposte? Why does everything have to be a snappy answer?

GUS.   Well. A little snap takes the sting out of reality. This being the *only* reality. And I've known *you* to snap out an answer in your time. The original riposte-woman. Even though tonight you're impersonating Hamlet the melancholy dame. But listen, if you want to take up philosophy, sort of a thoughtful hobby on top of an already lucrative career, I say go for it. I'll back you up, honey.

LAURA.   Okay, okay. I was being trite. So shoot me.

GUS.   I can't shoot you. You wouldn't exist anymore, and what would I do with all the furniture? We finally get a bigger apartment and she dies on me! Oh great! Thanks very much!

LAURA.   But you know what?

GUS.   What.

LAURA.   This pen still exists in my hand.

GUS and LAURA.   *In my living hand.*

LAURA.   Thank you.

GUS.   Maybe we could sell this to Parker Pens. "The new bottom-line fountain pen. Doesn't write very well — but it exists."

LAURA.   "To Bic or not to Bic."

GUS.   That's the spirit. You know what you need in your present mood? You need my new invention. Listen to this, you'll love it. *Two-D glasses.* You put them on and everything looks like a movie. Is that brilliant? Those days when the shit is hitting the fan at the speed of light, you just pop these on and, hey, no problem! I'm in a movie! Available in black-and-white, or technicolor for that gaudy MGM look. Perfect for somebody with reality jitters like yourself. What's the matter?

LAURA.   Nothing.

GUS.   Here's a philosophical speculation. Since you're in a philosophical mood. You know how the secret purpose of bees is to pollinate flowers? Has anybody ever thought the secret

15

purpose of human beings might be to pollinate furniture? I mean look. I sit down on a couch, I move to a dining-room chair, carrying some couch pollen on the backs of my thighs, maybe in the middle of the night a little divan quietly blossoms into being. Or maybe I sit in a chair, you sit in a chair, we change chairs, and a love-seat is born.

LAURA.   Could you be quiet for a minute? Please?

GUS.   I'm sorry. Was I babbling again?

LAURA.   I'm sorry.

GUS.   Well. You're in a rather somber and serious mood and I was feeling rather good. Just wanted to keep things lively.

LAURA.   Don't you sometimes ...

GUS.   What.

LAURA.   Sometimes I think I live in the world but I don't know anything about it. Even after all these years. I still don't know the first thing about the world. I don't know anything about anything! Lately some days I think my life's just going to go on and on like this. And then stop.

GUS.   Go on like what?

LAURA.   Well. Like this.

GUS.   What's "this"? And what's wrong with "this?"

LAURA.   No — nothing. I just ...

GUS.   We're doing great.

LAURA.   Sure.

GUS.   As always.

LAURA.   We're doing fine.

GUS.   Mmm. Not the most convincing reading of that line I've ever heard.

LAURA.   You yourself said "to *better* days."

GUS.   Oh come on, Laura.

LAURA.   Implying that everything isn't as perfect as it could be.

GUS.   I just meant— I didn't mean anything, I just ...

LAURA.   It's like tonight. We'll go out with Tony and Bea and we'll argue about which restaurant to go to — as if it was important — and then we'll talk about what movies we've all seen and we'll all be very clever and have a lot of snappy answers and then we'll discuss and compare the food we're eating and the food we've had this week and the food we're planning to eat and the movie reviews in the *Times*, and then we'll go home and everything will be exactly the same as it was until the next time we meet to talk about restaurants and movies.

GUS.   Well. There's nothing wrong per se with restaurants and movies. I mean, Szechwan cooking and bad foreign films are what make life worth living.

LAURA.   Mm.

GUS.   Laura, what is with you tonight? You're a dirge. You're the Brahms German *Requiem* when you ought to be a Rodgers and Hammerstein musical. We're moving out! This is no time for philosophy! I have seen the future and it's Riverside Drive! And it is going to be great!

LAURA.   What if they never find that woman?

GUS.   What?

LAURA.   This Ruth. What if it's never explained what happened to her? And she really does vanish without a trace?

GUS.   Help me out here. I think I missed a chapter.

LAURA.   Gus, maybe we shouldn't move.

GUS.   Shouldn't *move?* Wait a minute, Laura. Pump the brake slowly, we're sliding.

LAURA.   We've been in this place a long time. We like this place.

GUS.   We're moving. Okay? No. We *have moved.*

LAURA.   Why should we move?

GUS.   First of all we haven't been in this place all that long.

LAURA.   We've been here long enough.

GUS.   It's always been too small. And what about when little feet are pattering all around us? We'll need a lot more room then, whenever that happens, which as far as I understand we both hope will be relatively soon. Or am I right?

LAURA.   But this place —

GUS.   Yes. This place is us. This place will always be us and all the good times "us" have had here. We've also just spent a huge amount of time and trouble finding a *new* place that we like and can afford, and — I don't think you have reality jitters. You have moving panic. You know. That weird disjointed melancholy that settles over you right before you leave a place where you've been happy? But you can be happy in another place!

LAURA. Have you really been happy here?

GUS. Yes! I've been very happy here.

LAURA. Are you happy now?

GUS. Well no, not right *now*, right now I'm talking rather loudly trying to remind you that this is us, here. Remember? Us?

LAURA. And what is that?

GUS. You are going off your head, woman. And you're very quickly sending me off of mine.

LAURA. The night my father died.... And this was after they gave up hope on him and he knew he didn't have much time.... The night before he died he got into this ... panic, he started thrashing around in the bed and telling my mother to call the doctor. And all this time my mother sat there by the bed holding his hand and saying, "The doctor can't help you, Bill. The doctor can't help you anymore."

GUS. Laura, what can I do for you?

LAURA. Nothing.

GUS. Talk to me. What can I do?

LAURA. My father died this miserable ugly death screaming for a doctor and then vanished without a trace.

GUS. He didn't *vanish*, he ...

LAURA. My mother vanished. You and I will vanish too, along with a billion other people. Without a ripple.

GUS. Where did this cheery mood came from, anyway?

LAURA. Some days it's like my life is made of this incredibly thin white tissue, it's like a wall of very fine gauze. And the events from somebody's life are being projected on that fabric — and it's my life. Woman brushing her teeth. Woman sitting at her desk. And this membrane is so thin, it's like I could reach out and just push my finger right through it.

GUS. I don't know what to tell you.

LAURA. And what would I see if I could push through that fabric? What would I see on the other side?

GUS. I don't know. Probably New Jersey.

LAURA. Then suddenly I think — no. This is reality.

GUS. You know maybe you *do* need two-D glasses. You're halfway there already. In your case, maybe *one*-D glasses —

LAURA. Jesus Christ, Gus!

GUS. I'm sorry, I just — I'm trying to deal here. Laura, this is a mood, it's.... Nothing is different! We're the same people we were yesterday. You're just ...

LAURA. All my life — I guess I've just realized this too — all my life I've somehow taken it for granted that everything would be explained some day. Like I'd get to the last chapter and I'd find out who the killer was, a messenger would arrive and explain why this happened to me when I was twelve, or whatever happened to some ... book I lost when I was fifteen, and what this all meant. But that's never going to happen. You don't find these things out. You never find anything out.

GUS. Yes. Life is a mystery. That's very profound.

LAURA. Fuck you.

GUS. Fuck me? First go to hell, now fuck you. All in one night. Okay.

LAURA. *Fuck you.*

GUS. Laura, what the hell am I supposed to tell you? That everything *will* be explained someday? An angel's going to come down and hand you the winning envelope with the secret of life in it? I don't think that's going to happen. Or — okay — it *won't* be explained. I agree with you. We don't know anything about anything. We're idiots in a dark and mysterious universe. Does that make you feel better? *(Laura says nothing.)* Now what do you say we head over to Tony and Bea's and we won't talk about restaurants or movies. We'll talk about whatever you want. We'll talk philosophy.

LAURA. This is not ...

GUS. Okay.

LAURA. This is not philosophy, Gus. This is not a *mood.*

GUS. Okay.

LAURA. This is my life.

GUS. Yes.

LAURA. This is my life.

GUS.   And what can I do for you, to make your life better?
LAURA.   I just keep hearing my mother say that. "The doctor can't help you, Bill. The doctor can't help you anymore."
GUS.   Well. I will not be brought down. I refuse to be brought down. I was feeling so ... good, I.... How can I convince you that everything is good, that your life is good, that your life isn't any worse or different than it was yesterday?
LAURA.   Why don't you go and I'll wait for these people.
GUS.   Forget these people! Fuck 'em!
LAURA.   I'll finish packing. You go on.
GUS.   Okay. You finish packing.
LAURA.   I'm not that hungry anyway.
GUS.   Okay.
LAURA.   I'm lousy company tonight.
GUS.   Well. There's the CD player needs to be packed. You could tape up these boxes. *(He gets his coat.)* I'll call you before we go anywhere to tell you where we're going. In case you hear the call of Chow Fun. What's the matter now?
LAURA.   I just thought, you wouldn't have done this when we first met. Or even a year ago.
GUS.   What?
LAURA.   You would've stayed here and waited with me.
GUS.   I didn't mean to — I just wanted to — Oh, JESUS!
LAURA.   And I'm not saying that to accuse you, I just —
GUS.   What is that, a form of praise? A term of endearment? "You wouldn't have done that when we first met"?
LAURA.   I'm saying things change. Things were better.
GUS.   When?
LAURA.   Better days.
GUS.   You set me up, Laura.
LAURA.   I didn't set you up.
GUS.   You offered to stay and then you accuse me of abandoning you? I think that's pretty fucking mean.
LAURA.   That's not what I mean.
GUS.   Well maybe someday I'll get an explanation of what you mean. When I reach the last chapter and everything's explained. When the fucking messenger arrives. *(She says nothing.)* Okay. I'm going over there. I'll call you in a while.

LAURA.   'Bye.

GUS.   I think — Oh fuck it. We'll talk later. *(He exits up left. Laura sits on the box again and puts her face into her hands for a moment. Then she goes to the CD player against the wall at right and turns it on. Music comes on, softly. There is a knock at the door up left.)*

LAURA.   Gus —? *(Laura opens the door to Jack, 60, in a long, shabby coat with snowflakes on the shoulders.)* Oh. Hi. Sorry. I thought you were my husband.

JACK.   I was just wondering if I could look at your apartment.

LAURA.   Sure. Absolutely. Come on in. *(Jack hesitates.)* Really. Come in. *(Jack comes in.)*

JACK.   I'm sorry to bother you.

LAURA.   No. No bother. I knew you were coming sometime tonight.

JACK.   You knew I was coming...?

LAURA.   The agent told us. I'm Laura. And — I'm sorry — your name is...?

JACK.   Jack.

LAURA.   Hello, Jack. *(He looks around himself in silence a moment.)* Is it snowing out now? Looks like you've got snow on your coat. *(No response.)* Jack...?

JACK.   Yes. It's snowing out. *(He keeps looking about at the room.)*

LAURA.   You know somehow I thought there were going to be two of you. I mean, I thought they said a husband and wife ...

JACK.   No. It's just me.

LAURA.   Uh-huh. Well. This is the place. Living room. Obviously. Fireplace. Which doesn't work, unfortunately. Though some of the shutters still work. Then there's a bedroom and a small study down the hall, and a kitchen and bathroom off to the left. *(Jack is standing in the center of the room, very still, with his eyes closed.)* And that's pretty much it. If you want to take a look.

JACK.   God. God. *(Laura takes this in, a moment.)*

LAURA.   You know the rent is pretty steep. I don't know if

21

they made that clear. *(Jack says nothing, remaining perfectly still.)*
By the way — how did you get into the building? I mean it's
a pretty safe building, usually you have to buzz people in.

JACK. The fireplace doesn't work?

LAURA. Contrary to the ad. It did once. *(Jack says nothing.)*
But listen, Jack. I do have lots of things to do, we're right in
the middle of packing here, so I'm afraid I'm going to have
to let you go soon. My husband will be coming back in a second. And we can't go on meeting like this.

JACK. Fuck. Fuck. Fuck. Fuck.

LAURA. Jack, you're going to have to go now. *(He says nothing.)* I don't want to have to call somebody.

JACK. The fireplace used to work. And all the shutters. *(Indicating the wall up right.)* This was a doorway into the kitchen,
right here. Just a tiny little.... You couldn't open the refrigera-
tor and stand in the kitchen at the same time.

LAURA. So ... you used to live here, once upon a time.

JACK. *(Indicating the doorway, C.)* This was a bathroom,
through here. With a beautiful bright red door. Very red.

LAURA. Taking a trip down memory lane tonight, huh?

JACK. And this was the whole place. There weren't any
other rooms. This was it. And it seemed enormous. *(Pointing
to where the furniture had been.)* Couch. Chair. Rug over there,
Turkish rug. Table. Books. Books. And the bed, over here. *(He
goes to far left.)* This was where we used to make love. Right on
this spot. Right here. Right ... here. Nights like this we'd build
a fire and close up the shutters. Take our clothes off. Drink
wine and talk philosophy all night in bed. The meaning of
life. Do you understand? The meaning of life.

LAURA. Yes.

JACK. She found this old record we'd play over and over
and over again.

LAURA. "Long Ago and Far Away."

JACK. "Long Ago and Far Away." There was the whole rest
of the universe and this one little place, and the two of us
inside it. Warming our hands at each other. Everything led
right here, to this room and the two of us. Talking, talking,
talking.

LAURA.   About the meaning of life.

JACK.   It was paradise.

LAURA.   And she —? Where is she?

JACK.   Paradise ... *(Thoughtful now, Laura doesn't notice as Jack wanders out through the doorway at C. — where a bright red door appears, quietly closing shut. The music on the CD player fades out and we hear an old recording of "Long Ago and Far Away."* The CD player goes into the wall and is replaced by an old phonograph. Laura notices this and turns as a fire blazes up in the fireplace, and the wall up right opens, revealing a tiny kitchen. As Laura stands there looking at all this, the door up left opens and a Landlady steps in.)*

LANDLADY.   What's going on here? *(She goes to the record player and turns it off.)* How did you get in here?

LAURA.   Well I —

LANDLADY.   I didn't hear the doorbell. Who let you in?

LAURA.   Nobody. I was here.

LANDLADY.   You were here. And the fire? That started itself?

LAURA.   It did, actually.

LANDLADY.   Mm-hm. I suppose you're the one looking for the room.

LAURA.   Excuse me?

LANDLADY.   Are you here to look at the room? Well?

LAURA.   Um. Yes. I'm here to look at the room.

LANDLADY.   Well. This is the room. Sorry about the mess. The last tenants left all this behind. *(She indicates the boxes.)*

LAURA.   I don't understand ...

LANDLADY.   The people who lived here before left these things.

LAURA.   No, I understand that, but —

LANDLADY.   It's a single room studio apartment. Bathroom's through there. You got new plumbing and a new toilet and sink. You can see the kitchen through there. It's small, but everything works. I pay heat and water, you pay electric, rent is 80 dollars a month payable on the first. If you're interested,

---

* See Special Note on Music on copyright page.

I can give you an application. *(Laura just stares at her.)* I suppose you have references?

LAURA.   References.

LANDLADY.   Do you have a job? Are you working?

LAURA.   I did have a job. I'm not sure I have it anymore.

LANDLADY.   So you're out of work.

LAURA.   Well. I don't really know. *(Off her look.)* I'm not crazy.

LANDLADY.   It's always the crazy ones who say that. I see a ring there on your finger. This means you're married?

LAURA.   I have been married.

LANDLADY.   So where's your husband?

LAURA.   My husband sort of ... disappeared.

LANDLADY.   Mm. You got any kids, or...?

LAURA.   No. No kids.

LANDLADY.   So you're just looking for yourself.

LAURA.   Listen, do you mind if I just sit here for a minute? And think about all this?

LANDLADY.   I got some others coming to look, so if you want the room you'd better say so. I can't promise anything. And I can't wait forever. *(She starts out.)*

LAURA.   Yes.

LANDLADY.   Yes what.

LAURA.   I want the room. I'll take it.

LANDLADY.   You'll take the room. Just like that.

LAURA.   Well. I think I could be very happy here. The shutters work, don't they?

LANDLADY.   The shutters work. Everything.

LAURA.   I could put a couch here. A chair here. Turkish rug. Bed over here ... *(She stands at far left.)* Who knows. It could be paradise.

LANDLADY.   I'm going to need something in advance, if you don't have a job.

LAURA.   I can find a job. Really.

LANDLADY.   Well ...

LAURA.   I'm a very good tenant.

LANDLADY.   Why don't I get an application and we'll talk

24

about it. *(She starts out, but stops.)* And your name is —?

LAURA.   My name is Ruth.

LANDLADY.   Ruth. *(The Landlady goes out up left. Laura looks around at the place.)*

LAURA.   Yes, I think I could be very happy here ... *(She sees her wine glass, still half-full, sitting on the mantel. She picks it up, turns the record player back on, and "Long Ago and Far Away"* comes back on. She carries the wine glass into the kitchen and suddenly the wall closes as it had been before. The red door disappears at C. and the open doorway reappears, and the fire goes out in the fireplace. The record player is replaced by the CD player as that song fades out and the other music returns. The door up left opens and Gus comes in.)*

GUS.   Laura, look, I'm sorry — *(He sees that she's not there.)* Laura...? *(He is about to start into the doorway C., when Jack appears there, entering.)* Who're you? Are you the, to look at the apartment? I'm looking for my wife. She back there? *(Jack doesn't respond.)* Laura...? *(Gus goes out at C. and we hear him offstage.)* Laura? *(Jack stands at the place where the bed had been at far left. After a moment, Gus reenters.)* Where is she? Did she go out, or...?

JACK.   Would you take this? *(He hands Gus a white envelope.)* Give it to somebody?

GUS.   What is this...?

JACK.   That'll explain everything.

GUS.   The fuck is going on around here...? *(Jack has taken a pistol out of his coat. Jack puts the gun to his heart and fires. He falls. Gus backs off in shock, looking down at the body.)* Jesus. Jesus ... Laura?! *(He drops down onto the box where Laura was sitting at the beginning.)*

BLACKOUT

* See Special Note on Music on copyright page.

PROPERTY LIST

Pen (LAURA)
Box (GUS)
Record album (GUS)
Newspaper (GUS)
Coat (GUS)
Bottle of wine (GUS)
Glasses for wine (GUS)
CD player (LAURA)
Record player
Pistol (JACK)

FOREPLAY or:

The Art of the Fugue

this play is for Bennett Cohen

FOREPLAY OR THE ART OF THE FUGUE was presented at the Manhattan Punch Line Theatre (Steve Kaplan, Artistic Director), in New York City, in February, 1991. It was directed by Jason McConnell Buzas; the set design was by Vaughn Patterson; the costume design was by Kitty Leech; the lighting design was by Pat Dignan and the stage manager was Jim Williams. The cast was as follows:

AMY	Laura Dean
CHUCK I	Robert Stanton
PHYLLIS	Alison Martin
CHUCK II	Tony Carlin
ALMA	Anne O'Sullivan
CHUCK III	Brian Howe

CHARACTERS

AMY, early 20s, very sweet
CHUCK I, early 20s, very charming
ANNIE, mid-20s, very wry
CHUCK II, mid-20s, very smooth
ALMA, any age from early 20s to 30s; very sexy
CHUCK II, late 20s, pretty tired

All three Chuck's are dressed exactly the same.

SETTING

A bare stage representing a miniature-golf course. Upstage, a sign that says "LILLI-PUTT LANE."

NOTE: Actual golf balls are not used, though the motions are made of setting them down, putting, retrieving them from holes, etc.

FOREPLAY or:

The Art of the Fugue

At lights up: Chuck I and Amy, with golf clubs.

CHUCK I. *FORE!*

AMY. I can't believe I'm out here.

CHUCK I. Amy, you are going to fall in love tonight.

AMY. I am?

CHUCK I. With miniature golf.

AMY. Chuck ...

CHUCK I. I swear. This night will turn you into a miniature-golf-o-*maniac.* You're going to like this game so much, you'll wake up shorter tomorrow.

AMY. Very cute.

CHUCK I. Just remember one thing: miniature golf is bigger than you or me.

AMY. *(Setting a "ball" down.)* You must be some kind of a charmer, to talk me into this.

CHUCK I. So take your best shot and just try to resist. Go on.

AMY. Okay ...

CHUCK I. *(As she hits the ball.)* Puck! *(As it travels.)* Aaaaaaaaaaaaaaand — *(It misses.)* Ouch.

AMY. Ohhhhhhhhhhhh ... *(This disappointed, fading moan is the sound that Amy will typically make when she misses a shot.)*

CHUCK I. Too bad. Did you know, by the way, that a race of dwarves once covered the earth? *This* — *(The miniature-golf course.)* — is what they left behind.

AMY. Ha, ha.

CHUCK I. This was their Stonehenge.

AMY. Did you just think of this?

CHUCK I. You didn't know that but it's true.

AMY. Did you just make that up?

CHUCK I.   *(Motioning for her to proceed.)* But please.

AMY.   I don't know how I got into this.

CHUCK I.   *(As she putts again.)* Puck! Aaaaaaaaaaaaaand —
Ouch.

AMY.   *(Missing.)* Ohhhhhhhhhhhh ...

CHUCK I.   Nice bounce. But no cigar.

AMY.   It wasn't a *bad* shot.

CHUCK I.   Anyway, that's why I come out here to Lilli-Putt
Lane. To sense a cosmic connection with the ancient anthro-
pology of the game.

AMY.   Uh-huh. And to seduce girls.

CHUCK I.   *What?!*

AMY.   Oh come on, Chuck.

CHUCK I.   What guy in his right mind would take a girl
miniature-*golfing* to seduce her?

AMY.   You would. You've got quite a reputation, you know.

CHUCK I.   What, "reputation?"

AMY.   *Don Juan.*

CHUCK I.   Amy, I swear. I've never taken a girl miniature-
golfing in my life. Or anybody *else's* life!

AMY.   Uh-huh.

CHUCK I.   But do you want to take your next shot? I can
see you're getting hooked.

AMY.   *(Lining up the putt.)* If this is about getting into bed
with me ...

CHUCK I.   Never in a million years.

AMY.   You can think again.

CHUCK I.   *(As she putts.)* Puck! Aaaaaaaaaaaaaaaaand —

AMY.   *(As it goes in.)* Yes!

CHUCK I.   *Hey!* That was good, Amy!

AMY.   That was good, wasn't it?

CHUCK I.   That was *very* good.

AMY.   Wow! That felt *great!*

CHUCK I.   It's almost an erotic thrill, isn't it? *(Off her look.)*
I take it back. It's not an erotic thrill. It's a mild celibate
frisson.

AMY.   You are shameless.

CHUCK I.   *(Getting ready to putt.)* Quiet, please. I'm concentrating here. *(He tees off.) Puck!*

AMY.   *(As the ball travels.)* Mmmmmmmmmmmmmmmmmm-
mmmmm ...

CHUCK I.   *(Overlapping that.)* Aaaaaaaaaaaaaaaaaaaaaand ...
(The ball goes in.) BINGO!

AMY.   Wow!

CHUCK I.   Am I good?

AMY.   That was *nice!*

CHUCK I.   Am I good?

AMY.   You're really good.

CHUCK I.   Okay. Let's put this down for infinity. *(Marks a
scorecard.)* Three for Amy. And a hole in one ... for Chuck.

AMY.   God. It takes so little, doesn't it.

CHUCK I.   So little?

AMY.   To make people happy. It takes so little for happiness.

CHUCK I.   And what's littler than miniature golf? So are you
getting interested? Shall we play on?

AMY.   Yeah. Let's play on.

CHUCK I.   *FORE!*

CHUCK II.   *(Off-stage.) FORE! (As Chuck I and Amy move on
to the second hole, Chuck II enters with Annie at the first hole.)*

ANNIE.   Chuck, they ought to lock you up.

CHUCK II.   What...?

ANNIE.   You are *shameless,* Chuck.

CHUCK I.   This is nothing, you know.

AMY.   What.

CHUCK II.   Annie, *what?*

CHUCK I.   I once played miniature golf in Japan.

AMY.   In Japan?

ANNIE.   Oh, right.

CHUCK I.   Right there on the slopes of Mount Fuji.

CHUCK II.   I've never taken a girl miniature-golfing in my
entire life!

ANNIE.   I'll bet.

CHUCK II.   I swear!

CHUCK I.   I swear!

CHUCK II.   Or anybody *else's* entire life!

AMY.   Uh-huh.

CHUCK II.   You don't believe me?

ANNIE.   With your reputation?

CHUCK II.   What reputation?

ANNIE.   *Don Juan.*

CHUCK II.   Oh Amy, Amy. You have to learn to trust people.

CHUCK I.   *(As Amy gets ready to tee off again.)* Trust yourself, now.

ANNIE.   Annie.

CHUCK II.   Excuse me?

ANNIE.   My name is Annie. You called me Amy.

CHUCK II.   I'm sorry. *Annie.*

ANNIE.   *(Sets her "ball" down.)* I'm going to keep my eye on you.

CHUCK I.   *(To Amy.)* Just keep your eye on the ball.

CHUCK II.   Annie-way — prepare to fall in love tonight. With miniature golf.

ANNIE.   Oh yes?

CHUCK II.   This game is bigger than you or me, you know.

ANNIE.   Very clever. I just hope nobody *sees* me out here.

CHUCKS I and II.   *(As Amy and Annie tee off.) Puck!*

CHUCK II.   Aaaaaaaaand ...

CHUCK I.   Aaaaaaaaaaaaaand ...

AMY.   Mmmmmmmmmmmmmmmmmm ...

ANNIE.   *(Her typical sound, at missing a shot.) Nyugh!*

AMY.   Ohhhhhhhhhh ...

CHUCK I.   Too bad.

CHUCK II.   Nice lay, though.

CHUCK I.   Very nice lay.

CHUCK II.   *(Off Annie's look.)* It's a *golfing* term.

CHUCK I.   It's perfectly innocent.

AMY and ANNIE.   I'm sure. *(The women get ready to putt again.)*

CHUCK I.   But you know in Japan, the people are so short miniature golf is *really* miniature over there. Like this high. *(Ankle-height.)*

AMY.   Very cute.

CHUCK I.   You didn't know that, but it's true.

CHUCK II.   Did you know, by the way, that a race of dwarves once covered the earth? This is what they left behind.
ANNIE.   Ha, ha.
CHUCK II.   This was their Stonehenge.
ANNIE.   Very cute.
CHUCK II.   You didn't know that but it's true.
AMY.   I know you're only trying to distract me.
ANNIE.   You're not going to distract me.
CHUCK II.   Puck!
CHUCK I.   Puck!
CHUCKS I and II.   Aaaaaaaaaaaaand —
CHUCK II.   *(As Annie misses.)* BONG.
ANNIE.   *Nyugh!*
AMY.   Ohhhhhhhhhhh ...
CHUCK II.   Anyway, that's why I come out here. To sense a cosmic connection with my shorter predecessors.
AMY.   Did you just make all that up?
ANNIE.   Does somebody write all this for you?
CHUCKS I and II.   What?
AMY.   Golfing in Japan.
CHUCK II.   I don't make anything up.
CHUCK I.   This is truth!
ANNIE.   You do have ...
AMY.   There is *some*thing about you ...
ANNIE.   Charm. I guess.
CHUCK II.   I'm a very serious guy!
CHUCK I.   I'm a very serious guy, at heart.
AMY.   You sure have a way of making everything mean something else.
CHUCK I.   And that's exactly what I like about miniature golf.
CHUCK II.   Do you know what I like about this game?
CHUCK I.   It means something else.
CHUCK II.   It's a metaphor.
CHUCK I.   It's a great metaphor.
ANNIE.   Okay. A metaphor.
AMY and ANNIE.   What *for?*
AMY.   *I* know.

ANNIE.   For sex.

AMY.   For seduction.

CHUCK I.   No —

CHUCK II.   No —

ANNIE.   Sure. "Keeping *score.*"

AMY.   "Getting it in the hole."

CHUCK I.   No —

CHUCK II.   No —

CHUCK I.   No! It's a metaphor for *life!*

CHUCK II.   For *death.*

ANNIE.   Did you say "for *death?*"

CHUCK II.   Those aren't just *holes* out there.

CHUCK I.   These are stages on the journey of life.

CHUCK II.   The course always leads to the same final place.

CHUCK I.   But the course is different for everybody.

CHUCK II.   Sandtraps.

CHUCK I.   Waterholes.

CHUCK II.   The sands of time.

CHUCK I.   The oases of purification.

CHUCK II.   The final hole.

CHUCK I.   The verdant fairways ...

AMY.   What a beautiful idea!

ANNIE.   What a crock of manure!

CHUCK I.   And I believe it.

ANNIE.   Right. The five stages of miniature golf: anger, denial, grief, blame — and a windmill.

CHUCK II.   That's good, Amy.

CHUCK I.   You're a good person.

ANNIE.   Annie.

CHUCK II.   Annie.

CHUCK I.   Amy.

CHUCK II.   But maybe you're just *afraid* of the challenge of miniature golf.

ANNIE.   I'm afraid of the challenge of miniature *men.*

CHUCK II.   Ha!

CHUCKS I and II.   Play on?

AMY.   Yeah.

ANNIE.   Definitely.

AMY and ANNIE.   Let's play on.

CHUCK II.   Good.

CHUCKS I and II.   *(As the women putt.) Puck!*

CHUCK I.   Aaaaaaaaand ...

CHUCK II.   Aaaaaaaaaaaaand ...

AMY.   *(Joining in, overlapping.)* Mmmmmmmmmmmmmmmmm-mmmm ...

ANNIE.   *(Joining in, overlapping.)* Uhhhhhhhhhhhhhhhhhhhhh-hhhhh ...

AMY and ANNIE.   *YES!*

CHUCK II.   Nice shot.

CHUCK I.   Nice shot.

AMY.   Boy, that felt good!

ANNIE.   Whoo!

AMY.   Well!

ANNIE.   Wow. Thought I wasn't up to it, huh.

CHUCK I.   I told you you'd like it.

CHUCK II.   Maybe you only needed to ... handle the equipment.

ANNIE.   But the club is so small.

CHUCK II.   Ha, ha.

ANNIE.   Ho, ho.

AMY.   It really *is* an erotic thrill, isn't it?

CHUCK II.   Okay.

CHUCK I.   You want to see an erotic thrill?

CHUCK II.   Watch this.

CHUCKS I and II.   *(As they tee off, a soft sexual moan.) Mmmf.
(As the ball travels, the orgasm grows.)*

CHUCK I.   Oh, yes ...

CHUCK II.   Yes ...

AMY.   Mmmmmmmmmmmmmm ...

CHUCK I.   *Yes...!*

ANNIE.   Ohhhhhhhhhh ...

CHUCK II.   Yes!

CHUCK I.   YES!

AMY and ANNIE.   OHHHHHHHHHHHH!

CHUCK II.   *YES!*

CHUCK I.   *YES!*

CHUCKS I and II. *BINGO! (Collective fading postorgasmic moan.)*

AMY. Boy! Nice shot!

CHUCK I. Am I good?

CHUCK II. Am I good?

ANNIE. You're good, all right.

AMY. You're very good.

CHUCK II. Okay. Let's put this down for infinity. *(The two Chucks mark their scorecards.)* A hole in one ...

CHUCK I. *Another* hole in one ...

CHUCKS I and II. For Chuck.

CHUCK II. So are you enjoying yourself?

AMY. I'm having a very good time.

ANNIE. I *am* enjoying myself, in spite of myself.

CHUCK I. Good.

CHUCK II. It takes so little, you know. To make people happy. Amy —

ANNIE. Annie.

CHUCK II. Annie ...

CHUCK I. Have you ever thought that there's a design in our lives?

CHUCK II. Maybe there's something bigger than all this.

ANNIE. Polo?

AMY. *I* think so.

CHUCK II. And you could be a part of it.

CHUCK I. You could be a part of some greater design in my life.

CHUCK II. You're so different.

CHUCK I. You're so different, somehow.

CHUCK II. You're not just ... Annie-body.

ANNIE. Ha, ha.

CHUCK II. We could just forget golf, you know.

CHUCK I. We could just go over to my place. The night is young.

CHUCK II. The stars are out ...

ANNIE. And chuck the game?

AMY. Why don't we see who wins first.

ANNIE. Let's play on a little.

CHUCK I.   Okay.

CHUCKS I and II.   *FORE!*

CHUCK III.   *(Off-stage.) FORE! (Chuck III enters with Alma.)* Do you know I've never taken a girl miniature-golfing before?

ALMA.   Oh yeah, how come? I been on lots of minichure-golf dates. *(That stops Chuck III, a little.)*

CHUCK III.   Oh, really...?

ALMA.   Sure, I love minichure golf. I play it all the time.

CHUCK III.   *(Not too heartily.)* Well good ...

CHUCK II.   Did I tell you that I once played miniature golf in Japan?

ANNIE.   In Japan?

CHUCK II.   Yeah. Miniature golf is *really* miniature over there. *(Ankle height.)*

ANNIE.   Ha, ha.

CHUCK I.   *(Clearing his throat.)* Hem, hem.

AMY.   I know you're only trying to distract me.

CHUCK II.   *Hem, hem.*

ANNIE.   Very cute. May I play on now?

CHUCK II.   Please.

CHUCK III.   Did you know that a race of dwarves once covered the earth?

ALMA.   They *DID? Dwarfs?*

CHUCK III.   Well. Not really.

ALMA.   You mean like *midgets?* Were all over the *world?*

CHUCK III.   I was only kidding, actually.

ALMA.   Oh boy, you had me scared! But I bet if that was really true, they probably would've left something like this behind, huh? Like *Stonehenge* or something.

CHUCK III.   Yeah.

ALMA.   Wouldn't that be funny?

CHUCK III.   Mm. Hysterical.

ANNIE.   But why don't *you* go first.

AMY.   *You* go first this time.

CHUCK I.   All right.

CHUCK II.   Gladly.

ALMA.   You want to go first?

CHUCK III.   Be my guest. But just remember: this game is

bigger than either one of us.

ALMA.   Huh?

CHUCK III.   It's *bigger* than us. *Bigger...?*

ALMA.   Oh. "Bigger" than us.

CHUCK III.   Than us. Just a little joke. *(Chuck I, Chuck II, and Alma line up to tee off.)*

AMY.   *(Clearing her throat.)* Hem.

ANNIE.   *(Clearing her throat.)* Hem.

CHUCK II.   That's not going to work, you know.

AMY.   *(As Chuck I putts.)* Puck!

ANNIE.   *(As Chuck II putts.)* Puck!

CHUCK III.   *(As Alma putts.)* Puck!

CHUCKS I, II, and III.   Aaaaaaaaaaaaaaand ...

CHUCK I.   *(Misses.)* Oof.

CHUCK II.   *(Misses.)* Ouch.

AMY and ANNIE.   BONG.

ALMA.   *YES! A HOLE IN ONE! WAAAAAAAAAAAH!*

ANNIE.   Too bad.

AMY.   Nice try, though.

ALMA.   Was that good?

CHUCK III.   That was good, Amy.

ALMA.   Alma.

CHUCK III.   Huh?

ALMA.   My name is Alma, you called me Amy.

CHUCK III.   Oh. Sorry.

ALMA.   No problem. You want to shoot?

AMY and ANNIE.   *(As Chuck I and II putt again.)* Puck!

CHUCKS I and II.   Aaaaaaaaaaaaaaaand ...

CHUCK III.   You know what I like about miniature golf?

ALMA.   The metaphor?

AMY and ANNIE.   BONG.

ANNIE.   Too bad.

ALMA.   Do you like the life metaphor or the death metaphor?

CHUCK III.   Uh — well. Never mind.

AMY.   Nice try.

CHUCK III.   It's not important.

ALMA.   I just like this 'cause it's fun. Like sex or something.

You want to ... shoot?

CHUCK III.   Sure.

ANNIE.   *(As Chuck II putts.)* Puck!

AMY.   *(As Chuck I putts.)* Puck!

CHUCK III.   *(Putting.)* Puck!

CHUCK I.   *(Dully.)* And —

CHUCK II.   *(Not much verve.)* Bingo.

ALMA.   *(Raspberry.)* Ppllb.

AMY.   I wouldn't worry about it.

ANNIE.   You're right on par for the hole. *(Amy, Annie and Chuck III get ready to putt.)*

ALMA.   You've got quite a reputation, you know.

CHUCK III.   Who, me?

ALMA.   Yeah. As a Donald Juan.

CHUCK III.   Oh. A Donald Juan.

ALMA.   But you're gripping it wrong.

CHUCK III.   Excuse me?

ALMA.   Keep your thumbs down.

CHUCK III.   Oh. Thanks.

CHUCK I.   *(As Amy putts.)* Puck.

AMY.   *Yes!*

CHUCK II.   *(As Annie putts.)* Puck.

ANNIE.   Excellent!

CHUCK III.   *(As he putts.)* Puck.

ALMA.   *(Raspberry.)* Lousy lay, too. — That's a golfing term.

AMY and ANNIE.   Scorecard, please. *(Chucks I and II hand over their scorecards.)*

CHUCK III.   You know I once played miniature golf in Japan?

ALMA.   Must be pretty miniature, the people are so short.

CHUCK III.   Look, we haven't gone out *before*, have we?

ALMA.   No.

CHUCK III.   mean, we haven't played this course before, have we?

ALMA.   I don't think so.

AMY and ANNIE.   FORE!

CHUCK I.   So anyway.

CHUCK II.   What's your story, Annie?

CHUCK I.   What's your background?

CHUCK III.   Got any family?

AMY.   I have two brothers.

ANNIE.   Three sisters.

ALMA.   Two brothers, a sister, a step-sister, a half-brother, and my dog Barky.

CHUCKS I, II and III.   Uh-huh.

CHUCK I.   *(As he putts.)* Puck.

CHUCK II.   *(As he putts.)* Puck.

CHUCK III.   *(As he putts.)* Puck.

ALMA.   Do you have to make those noises?

CHUCK I.   Ouch.

CHUCK II.   Oof.

AMY and ANNIE.   *BONG.*

CHUCK III.   What noises?

ALMA.   You make noises while you golf.

CHUCK III.   Oh. Sorry.

ALMA.   Your shot again, Dick.

CHUCK III.   It's *Chuck.*

ALMA.   Oh. Sorry. *(Chucks I, II and III prepare to putt again.)*

AMY.   Anyway ...

ANNIE.   My mother's dead.

AMY.   My father lives in Arkansas.

ALMA.   My brother is an undertaker.

CHUCKS I and II.   Puck!

AMY and ANNIE.   Aaaaaaaaaaaaaand —

ALMA.   My sister is a dike.

AMY and ANNIE.   *BONG!*

ALMA.   *(As Chuck III misses. Raspberry.)* Ppllb.

CHUCK III.   You know, *you* make noises too.

ALMA.   I do?

CHUCK III.   Oh yeah.

ALMA.   Funny. *I* never noticed.

CHUCK II.   So this brother ...

CHUCK I.   How old is your sister?

ANNIE.   I don't have a brother.

AMY.   It's two brothers.

CHUCK III.   So your mother is dead?

42

ALMA.   No, she's a beautician.

CHUCK I.   But your father is a carpenter?

CHUCK II.   Your mother lives in Michigan?

CHUCK III.   And you're divorced?

AMY, ANNIE and ALMA.   No!

AMY.   He's a pickle-packer.

ANNIE.   Buried in Kansas.

ALMA.   But I do have a boyfriend in the Navy.

CHUCKS I, II and III.   Oh. *(They putt.)*

AMY and ANNIE.   Puck!

CHUCKS I and II.   Aaaaaaaaaaaaaand — !

AMY, ANNIE, CHUCKS I and II.   BINGO!

ALMA.   *(Raspberry.)* Ppllb.

CHUCK III.   You know I can't hit the ball if I don't go "puck."

ALMA.   "Puck?"

CHUCK III.   I have to make a noise if I'm going to hit it right.

ALMA.   Oh. Okay. Make a noise.

CHUCK III.   It's my nature.

ALMA.   Okay.

CHUCK III.   I'm used to it.

ALMA.   Go ahead. Make all the noise you want.

CHUCK I.   *(Referring to Chuck III.)* Looks like we've got a real moron up ahead here.

CHUCK III.   *(Feeling Alma watching him.)* You're not going to make me miss my shot.

ALMA.   It's two inches away! Just hit it!

CHUCKS I and II.   *Playing through!*

CHUCK III.   Puck.

CHUCKS I and II.   *Playing through!*

CHUCK III.   And bingo.

AMY.   Okay, now.

ANNIE.   This is *war*.

AMY, ANNIE, CHUCKS I and II.   *(As Amy and Annie putt.)* Puck!

CHUCKS I and II.   Aaaaaaaaaaaaaand ...

AMY and ANNIE.   All right!

AMY, ANNIE, CHUCKS I and II. *(As Chuck I, Chuck II, and Alma putt.)* Puck!

AMY and ANNIE. Aaaaaaaaaaaaaaand ....

CHUCKS I and II. BINGO!

ALMA. *Yes! ANOTHER HOLE IN ONE! WAAAAAAAH!* — Want to shoot?

CHUCK I and AMY. Puck!

AMY. Ohhh ...

CHUCK II and ANNIE. Puck!

ANNIE. Nyugh!

ALMA. Pork! — *(Raspberry.)* Ppllb.

CHUCK III. It's "puck."

ALMA. Oh. Sorry.

AMY and ANNIE, CHUCKS I, II, and III. *(Operatic, Wagnerian.)* PUCK!

CHUCK I. Ouch.

CHUCK II. Oof.

ANNIE. Nyugh.

AMY. Yes.

CHUCKS I and II. Bingo!

ANNIE. Aaaaaaaaaaand ...

AMY. Aaaaaaaaaaaaand ...

CHUCK I. Aaaaaaaaaaaaaaaand ...

CHUCK II. Aaaaaaaaaaaaaaaaaaand ...

ALMA. *(Raspberry.)* Ppllb.

AMY, ANNIE, CHUCKS I and II. *(Wagnerian.)* PUCK!

CHUCK II. Ouch.

CHUCK I. Oof.

ANNIE. Yes!

AMY. Ohhhhhhh...! *(Crescendo to very loud.)*

CHUCK II. Aaaaaaaand ...

CHUCK I. Aaaaaaaaaaand ...

AMY. Mmmmmmmmmmmmmmm ...

ANNIE. Mmmmmmmmmmmmmmmmmm ...

CHUCKS I and II. AAAAAAAAAAAAAAAAAAAAAAAND —

AMY and ANNIE. MMMMMMMMMMMMMMMMMMMM —

CHUCK III. *(Quietly.)* Bingo.

AMY and ALMA, CHUCKS I, II, and III.   YES!

CHUCK I.   Okay, so where do we come out?

CHUCK II.   What's the score?

CHUCK III.   *(Exhausted.)* Are we done yet?

ANNIE.   Sorry, Chuck.

AMY.   You win. *(Falls into his arms.)*

ANNIE.   You lose. *(Shows him the scorecard.)*

CHUCK III.   Don't tell me. I lost.

ALMA.   You didn't lose. We got nine more holes.

CHUCK III.   The nine circles of hell.

ALMA.   Well listen. You wanna fuck?

CHUCK III.   I resign.

BLACKOUT

SEVEN MENUS

This play is for STEVE KAPLAN,
with tactless gratitude

SEVEN MENUS was presented by the Manhattan Punch Line Theatre, in New York City, in January, 1989. The production was directed by Fred Sanders; the set was by James Wolk; lighting was by Danianne Mizzy; costumes were by Fontilla Boone; sound was by Scott David Sanders; the assistant director was David Newman; and the production stage manager was Jay McManigal. The cast was as follows:

PAUL	Peter Basch
HAZEL	Melissa Weil
RUTH	Tessie Hogan
JACK	Michael Piontek
BARRY	Gary Cookson
DAWN	Debra Stricklin
PHYLLIS	Nancy McDonald
FLUFF	David Konig

At certain performances, the parts of Hazel and Dawn were played by Janine Robbins and Sandra La Vallee, respectively.

SEVEN MENUS

SCENE ONE

A restaurant booth. Jack, Ruth, Hazel, and Paul. All in their early thirties. Reading menus.

PAUL.   So why do they call this place Seven Menus?

HAZEL.   I really like this place, Ruth.

RUTH.   I thought you would.

PAUL.   There's only one menu.

HAZEL.   *("Peculiar.")* "Interesting" decor.

RUTH.   Jack introduced me.

JACK.   I like to think of this as a higher order of coffee shop. A sort of a ... transcendental diner.

HAZEL.   Well it's the first menu I've ever seen that says "Substitutions *Welcomed.*"

PAUL.   Shouldn't we ask for the other six?

HAZEL.   The other six what.

PAUL.   The other six menus.

JACK.   Paul.

PAUL.   Huh?

JACK and RUTH.   *What happened? (This is an old bit between these two, which they always use as if to say "Paul — wake up.")*

PAUL.   I knew they were going to say that.

JACK.   What happened, Paul?

PAUL.   I knew you two were going to say that.

JACK.   We always know exactly what we're going to say.

RUTH.   That's the great part.

JACK.   It is?

RUTH.   Well it's *part* of the great part.

51

JACK. The other part we'll save for later. *(They kiss.)*
HAZEL. Cool it, lovebirds. We've got health regulations to watch out for here.
PAUL. I don't get it.
HAZEL. Are you still searching for the lost menu?
PAUL. Yeah. Why Seven Menus if there's only one?
HAZEL. Maybe it's a translation.
PAUL. Whatever happened to truth in advertising?
HAZEL. Maybe "seven menus" is Chinese for happiness or something.
PAUL. But the place isn't Chinese. I can't tell *what* it is.
JACK. That's what they'll say about you someday, you know.
RUTH. About me?
JACK. You're in advertising, aren't you?
RUTH. I am indeed.
JACK. They'll say whatever happened to Ruth in advertising?
HAZEL. Ouch. Ouch.
JACK. Sorry.
PAUL. Who owns this place, anyway?
JACK. Greeks.
JACK and RUTH. Of course.
RUTH. Greeks own all restaurants everywhere.
JACK. After inventing tragedy all that was left was food services.
PAUL. This is all going too fast for me.
HAZEL. Well who wants what? Let's order.
RUTH. Will you look at that menu?
HAZEL. Cajun kielbasa? Char soo with beansprouts ...
JACK. And Billie Holiday on the jukebox.
PAUL. What's "joyau de la chasse?"
JACK. You got me.
HAZEL. "Joy of the chase?"
RUTH. Crown of the chase. Wild fowl stuffed with venison.
JACK. How did you know that?
RUTH. I don't know. Doesn't everybody know that?
JACK. *I* didn't know that.
HAZEL. She must've had it with some other guy, Jack.
JACK. I guess so.

HAZEL. Well I want a salad.

RUTH. Pastrami on rye for me.

JACK. *(Who has begun nibbling one of Ruth's fingers.)* I think I want just this one digit ...

RUTH. Finger food, huh.

PAUL. You know what I've got a taste for? French toast.

HAZEL. For *supper?*

PAUL. Actually it's the syrup. What I really want is some sugar.

HAZEL. Well it's a change, anyway.

PAUL. Only there's no French toast on the menu.

JACK. So order another menu.

PAUL. Where *are* the other menus?

HAZEL. Do you know that all the time we were dating, no matter what time of day it was, all Paul would ever order was meatloaf with gravy, mashed potatoes and peas? Every date we ever went out on, morning, noon or night.

PAUL. Or maybe some pancakes ...

JACK. So Paul used to be a real meatloaf-and-potatoes kinda guy.

RUTH. Now all he wants is sugar.

JACK. It's a sad change.

RUTH. *I* saw it coming.

HAZEL. Anyway, he'd mix the peas in with the mashed potatoes, then swirl in the gravy and sort of beat the meatloaf into submission, then stir the whole mess around on his plate till it was practically soup. And then he'd use a *tablespoon* to eat this goo.

JACK. Does his therapist know about this?

RUTH. I can't believe you married a guy who did things like that, Hazel.

JACK. Sick, baby.

PAUL. What about waffles? Do you think they have waffles at this place?

JACK. They have everything at this place.

PAUL. Everything but what I want.

RUTH. When do you guys leave for the Cape?

PAUL. Saturday morning, ten sharp.

RUTH. Well! *That* sure raised you out of your usual lethargy.

PAUL. You guys should come up and see the house.

JACK. I'd be outclassed.

PAUL. You can test the undertow.

HAZEL. You know, Ruth, I saw Scott when I was up in Providence.

RUTH. Oh yeah? How was that?

JACK. Should I leave the table?

HAZEL. Sit down.

RUTH. Did you talk to him?

HAZEL. Are you kidding? I gave him hell.

RUTH. No.

HAZEL. Not really.

JACK. I think I *will* leave the table.

RUTH. Oh sit down, Tristan.

HAZEL. I said that Ruth had hooked up with this terrific guy named Jack ... *(Jack whistles nonchalantly, as if to drown out her words.)* ... and that she was very happy ...

JACK. This is excruciating.

HAZEL. ... and that he — i.e., Scott — was past past past. Imperfect.

JACK. Did you say a terrific but penniless guy named Jack?

HAZEL. No, I just said terrific.

RUTH. It's all right, darling, I'll pay your check.

HAZEL. I don't know why you should find this excruciating.

JACK. Because I could be him someday. People sitting around and calling me a jerk, and me without the girl.

HAZEL. He *was* a jerk.

JACK. Just reminds you, a little, of the transience of love.

RUTH. Love? Transient?

JACK. You know what I studied in college, don't you?

HAZEL. I'm afraid to ask.

JACK. Romance Languishes.

HAZEL. Oof.

PAUL. That's pretty funny.

RUTH. So what did he say? When you talked to him.

HAZEL.   Nothing. Just *looked* at me. You know.

RUTH.   I can just see it.

JACK.   Now I *am* leaving the table.

HAZEL.   Oh sit down. We're all adults here.

JACK and RUTH.   We are?

HAZEL.   Yeah. Believe it or not, kids, this is adult life.

JACK.   Everybody else has three bank accounts and a house in the country.

RUTH.   *I* don't have a house in the country.

JACK.   But you *will* have a house in the country.

RUTH.   Money isn't everything, you know.

JACK.   It isn't?

RUTH.   No it's not.

JACK.   Thank God! *(They kiss.)*

PAUL.   Does anybody else want waffles?

HAZEL.   *(Sighs.)* True love. Isn't it wonderful? *(A bell rings. They freeze as they are for a moment. Jack Exits and Barry Enters and takes his place next to Ruth. Another bell rings.)*

SCENE TWO

PAUL.   But how's the big deal going, Barry?

BARRY.   It's going great.

PAUL.   Really?

BARRY.   We close on it the end of this week.

PAUL.   Terrific.

HAZEL.   Did you get the price you wanted?

BARRY.   *Better* than we wanted.

HAZEL.   Sure must be wonderful being with somebody who deals in zillions all day.

BARRY.   Parts-of zillions, anyway.

HAZEL.   A part of a zillion goes a long way.

RUTH.   Hang out with somebody in high finance for a while, Hazel. That'll teach you how little you know about the world.

BARRY.   So how come they call this place Seven Menus?

There's only one menu here.

PAUL. It's part of the place's mystique.

RUTH. Hegel wrestled with that question for years.

HAZEL. So did Kierkegaard.

BARRY. Hegel what?

PAUL. Hasn't Ruth brought you in here before, Barry?

BARRY. No, but I've heard so much about the place I feel like a regular already.

HAZEL. We've been coming in here with Ruth and — uh, with Ruth for a long time.

BARRY. Well I'm sure hungry.

PAUL. I'm starving.

RUTH. Who's going to have what?

PAUL. I want something with some sugar.

HAZEL. I feel like having something different ...

BARRY. What's good on this menu?

HAZEL. The other six menus.

BARRY. So what do I do with *this* menu?

HAZEL, PAUL and RUTH. Order another menu.

BARRY. What?

PAUL. Order another menu when the waiter comes. I went through this once myself, Barry.

RUTH. It's an ancient routine. *(Barry suddenly starts to laugh.)*

BARRY. Do you know we had a guy come in this past week with a suitcase full of money?

PAUL. Into your office?

BARRY. Yeah, just walked into the office with a suitcase full of dough. Fifties and hundreds, just laying there loose. Marches in, opens the case, shows them to the receptionist.

HAZEL. Did she offer marriage?

BARRY. No, she called me out there.

HAZEL. Did *you* offer marriage?

RUTH. No, listen to the rest of this. It's incredible.

BARRY. So he shows me all this money. There must've been fifty-sixty thousand dollars in this briefcase.

PAUL. I thought it was a suitcase.

BARRY. No, it was a leather briefcase.

PAUL. I thought you said suitcase.

HAZEL. There's a lot of difference between a suitcase and a briefcase full of money.

RUTH. Several years in prison, I think.

BARRY. Anyway, he wanted us to do something with all this money. Comes in off the street and just asks us to *do* something with all this money. He didn't even know what! *(Small pause.)*

HAZEL. So what did you do?

BARRY. Are you kidding? Kicked his ass back out in the street!

HAZEL. Seems a peculiar thing to do to a person with a briefcase full of money ...

BARRY. Who knows where he got all that dough. Could've been drugs, embezzlement, who knows.

HAZEL. I figure if somebody walks in with a suitcase or even a briefcase full of happiness, just grab it and run.

BARRY. No such luck, Hazel. Money is never just money.

RUTH. But isn't that incredible?

HAZEL. Yeah ...

PAUL. That settles it.

RUTH. What.

PAUL. A hot fudge sundae.

HAZEL. I'm glad to see you're still concentrating on the essentials.

BARRY. Guess it's that time, huh. *(Scans the menu, humming as he goes.)* Dadadadadadadadadadadadadadadada think I'll try the meatloaf.

RUTH and HAZEL. *Uh-oh!*

HAZEL. Meatloaf alert!

BARRY. What's so funny? What's everybody laughing about?

RUTH. Nothing. Just don't mix the meatloaf in with the vegetables.

BARRY. Why not?

HAZEL. Look what happened to us.

PAUL. Private joke, Bare.

RUTH. Paul used to use meatloaf as a sort of mating dance before they got married, that's all.

BARRY. Oh.

RUTH.   So there's your warning, hun.

BARRY.   Maybe I better go for breast of chicken and play it safe.

HAZEL.   Well *I'm* going to try the Welsh rarebit.

PAUL.   Hot fudge for me.

RUTH.   I'm going to go the whole hog and do the turkey dinner.

BARRY.   Actually, speaking of such things ...

RUTH.   Turkeys?

BARRY.   Mating dances.

HAZEL.   What.

BARRY.   *(To Ruth.)* Should we tell them?

RUTH.   You mean now?

BARRY.   Why not.

HAZEL.   Wake up, Paul.

PAUL.   What's going on?

HAZEL.   I think something's on the way.

RUTH.   *(To Barry.)* You or me?

BARRY.   Ruth and I are going to get married.

HAZEL.   Hooray!

PAUL.   Hey, that's terrific, you guys.

HAZEL.   Gimme kiss. *(She and Ruth kiss.)*

PAUL.   Congratulations, that's really terrific.

BARRY.   Thank you. Thank you. Thank you.

HAZEL.   I've seen this coming for minutes. *Months.*

PAUL.   When's the date?

RUTH.   We don't know yet.

BARRY.   I say the sooner the better.

RUTH.   That's so it doesn't interfere with all these deals.

HAZEL.   Oh hell, it's just a *marriage*. Run down the road and shanghai the first J.P. you can find.

RUTH.   My mother is hysterical.

RUTH and HAZEL.   *(Together.)* Of *course*.

HAZEL.   Well I say here's to it. Raise your water glasses, everybody.

BARRY.   My glass is dirty.

HAZEL.   Raise it anyway. To marriage, and all the rest of it.

ALL.   To marriage! *(Bell. They freeze as they are a moment. Hazel exits and Dawn, 24, Enters and takes her place next to Paul. Ruth takes out a book and reads. Another bell.)*

SCENE THREE

PAUL. Anyway I was thinking that after the wedding Dawn and I could do a week at the Cape, then a week just driving around, then maybe take a couple of weeks in Florida with her parents and get in some scuba diving.

BARRY. You've really shaken Paul out of his usual lethargy, Dawn. He's a totally new man.

DAWN. *(Southern accent.)* I guess I'm just an activity-oriented person by nature.

BARRY. He used to be practically comatose, till you came along. Paul — *what happened,* huh? What happened?

DAWN. But you know what all that lethargy was.

BARRY. What was that.

DAWN. It was all that sugar! That's why Paul's always been so low-energy. It was a sugar O.D.

PAUL. Now I'm off sugar I'm a dynamo.

BARRY. You sure look trim.

PAUL. Do I look trim?

RUTH. I didn't know you could scuba-dive, Paul.

PAUL. Huh?

RUTH. I said I didn't know that you could scuba-dive.

PAUL. Dawn's going to teach me.

DAWN. I love scuba-diving. I've been doing it since, God, since I was about *ten.*

RUTH. So you're still using the house on the Cape?

PAUL. What, me?

RUTH. Yeah. I thought ...

PAUL. No, Hazel and I split it up. Half a month each.

BARRY. That's a fair arrangement.

PAUL. Yeah, it all works out okay.

BARRY. That's very equitable.

DAWN. It's the least she could do, you know. .

RUTH.   I beg pardon?

DAWN.   Hazel. I mean she and Paul bought the house together, fifty-fifty. And you don't want 'em to just sell it, right?

RUTH.   Mm.

PAUL.   Anyway, you two guys'll have to come up for a weekend.

BARRY.   There's an idea.

DAWN.   Yeah, come up and test the water.

PAUL.   Get a change of air.

BARRY.   Or you two could come up to our place.

DAWN.   Do you have a house too?

PAUL.   They've got a *real* country house.

BARRY.   Up in the mountains.

DAWN.   Oh I *love* the mountains.

BARRY.   Southern Vermont.

DAWN.   I *love* Vermont.

BARRY.   Do you like to ski?

RUTH.   She *loves* to ski.

DAWN.   I *do* love to ski.

BARRY.   *(To Ruth.)* Hey.

RUTH.   What. Something wrong?

DAWN.   What's the matter?

BARRY.   Nothing.

RUTH.   Must've been something I ate. Not enough sugar or
something.

BARRY.   Maybe if you put the goddamn book down ...

PAUL.   You know what I'm going to have?

DAWN.   You don't even have to tell me.

PAUL.   Meatloaf and potatoes and gravy.

DAWN.   I knew it!

PAUL.   With peas.

DAWN.   I knew it! Everytime we go out, night or day, it's
always meatloaf and mashed potatoes and peas.

RUTH.   And then he mashes them all together on his plate?
Mixes the peas into the potatoes and stirs it all around?

DAWN.   How did you know?

RUTH.   Womanly intuition. But maybe you'll get a *quarter* of
the house on the Cape. Someday.

DAWN. What's she talking about?

PAUL. Just a private joke.

DAWN. A quarter of the house...?

BARRY. What do you do for a living, Dawn?

DAWN. I'm a food therapist.

RUTH. A *food therapist?*

DAWN. Uh-huh. So I treat things like obesity, and anorexia, and — you know — things like that.

BARRY. Sounds fascinating.

DAWN. I think it's a terrific way of finding out what makes people tick.

RUTH. Or burp, I suppose.

PAUL. You should hear some of her stories. Like this guy who was so fat he had to have his bed reinforced so he didn't just disappear right through the floor.

DAWN. That was due to a gland condition, though.

PAUL. Guy could've ended up in China!

DAWN. There was nothing the man could do about it since it was all glandular.

BARRY. Incredible.

DAWN. Everything is glands when you get right down to it.

RUTH. Are we about ready to order?

PAUL. Or this condition called bloomonia?

DAWN. Bulimia.

PAUL. Where people go on eating binges and then make themselves throw up?

RUTH. Do you think we could save bulimia for after dessert?

PAUL. Sure. Sure.

BARRY. Well who wants what?

DAWN. I haven't even had time to study this menu.

PAUL. Meatloaf for me.

DAWN. They have *pheasant* here?

PAUL. They have everything here.

RUTH. Here's something. *(Refers to her book.)* New statistics. Single women live longer than married women.

DAWN. Wow.

PAUL. Really?

DAWN. So single women live longer than married women?

RUTH. I think I just said that. But listen to *this* — (*She is about to read more from her book.*)

BARRY. (*Interrupting.*) Oh come on.

RUTH. Come on what.

BARRY. You ought to be able to see through that.

RUTH. See through what.

BARRY. You're in advertising, you know how to juggle figures. You can crunch a bunch of numbers any way you want.

DAWN. What else does it say?

RUTH. It says that single women are also overwhelmingly happier than married women.

DAWN. I didn't know that.

BARRY. Happy according to who?

RUTH. Happy according to themselves.

BARRY. Here's a woman hauling down a huge salary every year who can't see through a lot of crooked figures.

RUTH. Are we going to order? If we're not, I've got things to do at home.

BARRY. Just hold your horses, okay? Hold your horses. We'll order.

DAWN. You know, I was sitting on the bus the other day reading this book of stories, and I was laughing out loud —

PAUL. That book you read to me from?

DAWN. — yeah, and I was laughing really hard, and there was this guy sitting next to me, kind of an old guy, and he says, "Whatcha reading," and I said, "Stories."

BARRY. He was probably trying to pick you up.

DAWN. But listen to this. He says, "Looks like those stories are pretty funny," and I said some of them were funny, and *then* he says: "Have you got any heartrending ones in there?" (*Pause.*)

BARRY. Huh.

DAWN. Isn't that funny?

PAUL. "Have you got any heartrending ones in there ..."

DAWN. I thought it was kind of sad.

BARRY. Yeah. (*Pause. *)

PAUL. How's business with you, Barry?

BARRY.   Oh, you know. Nothing ever changes. *(Bell. Ruth and Paul leave. Dawn joins Barry on his side of the table, and he puts an arm around her. Phyllis sits at the table, smoking a cigarette. Fluff stands behind her. Bell.)*

SCENE FOUR

BARRY.   But once in a while you want something different.

DAWN.   We sure don't do this all the time, you know.

BARRY.   You want to try something new.

DAWN.   In fact we've never done it before in all our lives.

BARRY.   New faces, new bodies, new sensations.

DAWN.   I never even *read* those swinger magazines.

BARRY.   Makes for a little sauce, you know what I mean?

DAWN.   I mean, isn't it a little strange, advertising yourself for sex?

BARRY.   *(Referring to Fluff.)* Does your, uh, friend want to sit and join the party, or...?

PHYLLIS.   You two don't have any serious social diseases, do you?

DAWN.   Social dis —?

BARRY.   What, social diseases?

DAWN.   Oh no. No. I've never had a single thing like that.

BARRY.   I had the clap a couple of times in college, but who didn't?

FLUFF.   Do you have a very large penis?

BARRY.   Excuse me?

FLUFF.   Your penis. I have to watch out for my friend here.

DAWN.   But here we are talking about penises and we don't even know your names!

FLUFF.   I'm Simon.

PHYLLIS.   No he's not.

FLUFF.   I'm Charlie.

PHYLLIS.   No he's not.

FLUFF.   I am the Catch of the Day.

PHYLLIS.   I'm Phyllis and he's Fluff.

BARRY. "Fluff" — ?

FLUFF. Yeah. *(Shows four fingers.)* Three f's.

BARRY. Kind of an interesting name.

FLUFF. Anglo-Saxon.

DAWN. *(Quasi-confidentially, to Phyllis.)* Is he part of our — you know — liaison?

PHYLLIS. He's along for the ride.

BARRY. So are you guys gonna eat ... or shall we retire for some fun?

PHYLLIS. You're going to have to do a lot better than that. *(Picks up the menu.)* Seven Menus, huh ...

BARRY. Yeah, you noticed the name? It's a part of the place's mystique. Hegel once wrote a book about why they call this place Seven Menus.

FLUFF. There's no mystery about the name.

BARRY. I beg pardon?

FLUFF. You get a different menu depending on when you come in here.

BARRY. But I've been in here all hours of the day and it's always the same menu.

FLUFF. Sure. But *you're* different.

BARRY. Huh?

FLUFF. You're not the same person at supper that you were at breakfast. Breakfast, brunch, lunch, afternoon snack, cocktails, supper and midnight munch. These are the Seven Ages of Man. *(Pause.)*

DAWN. Didn't your ad say that you're in advertising?

PHYLLIS. Yeah, I run an ad agency.

DAWN. That must be great!

PHYLLIS. It has it moments. How's the pastitsio?

BARRY. It's good, it's good. I never tried it, but everything is good here.

DAWN. I always kind of wished I went into advertising when I had the chance.

BARRY. Do we need to talk about advertising? Let's talk about your-place-or-ours.

DAWN. Barry's ex used to be in advertising.

PHYLLIS. Really.

DAWN.   God she was a terrible person.
BARRY.   Yeah well ...
FLUFF.   I always liked her, actually.
DAWN.   Barry's ex?
FLUFF.   Yeah. I thought she was terrific.
DAWN.   Did you know her?
FLUFF.   Warm. Funny. Vulnerable. Lemon-flavored. Static-free. I still miss the bitch, to tell you the truth.
DAWN.   What *are* you? I mean — what do you do for a living?
FLUFF.   I don't do anything. I live off of her.
BARRY.   Is that for real?
PHYLLIS.   Uh-huh.
BARRY.   Nice work if you can get it.
PHYLLIS.   But he also knows the true meaning of tenderness.
BARRY.   I'm in the middle of a career change, myself.
DAWN.   He got fired.
BARRY.   I used to be in high finance, but lately I've been thinking I might go into food services.
FLUFF.   *Food services ...*
BARRY.   Yeah.
DAWN.   Anyway, how did you —
BARRY.   Food services is a very, very, interesting field.
DAWN.   But how did you get to run a whole agency?
BARRY.   Dawn here is in food therapy. I was thinking she and I could team up. I could cater the food and she could provide the therapy, after.
FLUFF.   Brilliant.
BARRY.   Just stay away from high finance, that's my advice.
DAWN.   Oh Barry ...
BARRY.   You get into some weird deals, and you are gone, buddy.
DAWN.   Are we gonna order now?
BARRY.   You know one time a guy came into our office with a couple of hundred thousand dollars in a suitcase?
DAWN.   Oh come on, Bare.
BARRY.   What, come on.

DAWN.   Not that story.

BARRY.   What story.

DAWN.   He tells this story all the time. About this guy who brought in some money in a briefcase.

BARRY.   A suitcase.

DAWN.   Okay, a suitcase.

FLUFF.   So what happened?

BARRY.   Nothing happened. It's not important.

FLUFF.   No really. What happened?

BARRY.   Nothing happened. We kicked the guy out. End of story. *(Bell. Barry and Fluff exit. Jack enters and sits next to Phyllis. Bell.)*

SCENE FIVE

DAWN.   But that's not the end of the story. Because I marched in there, and I put my hands on his desk and I said, *Advertising is about making choices.*

PHYLLIS.   *(Who does not smoke during this scene.)* Ten points.

DAWN.   Was I not a food therapist? Did I not design diets for people? And what are diets all about?

PHYLLIS.   Making the right choices.

DAWN.   So who's the best person for this account?

PHYLLIS.   You are.

DAWN.   And he gave it to me right on the spot. A million-dollar account!

PHYLLIS.   And she lived happily ever after.

DAWN.   You never should've left the agency, Phil.

PHYLLIS.   Ohhh no ...

DAWN.   Just think what you could be doing now.

PHYLLIS.   I'm very happy as a housewife, thank you.

DAWN.   Nobody's happy as a housewife.

PHYLLIS.   I have found my counter-revolutionary niche — roasting meat on a spit for a man who always comes home.

DAWN.   I thought that I'd found *my* niche, and God was I wrong! Do you know I ran into one of my old patients in the street the other day and I couldn't even remember his name? God I was so embarrassed. Sometimes I wonder how I could stand spending eight and ten hours a day with those people.

PHYLLIS.   I ran into an old boyfriend last week and I couldn't remember his name.

DAWN.   You're kidding. A client I can believe, but a *boyfriend?*

PHYLLIS.   Well — life is long, men short. In all too many cases. Not *all* men though. *(Nudges Jack, who has not been paying attention during all this, staring around himself at the restaurant.)* I'm talking about you, Jack.

JACK.   Oh. Sorry.

DAWN.   What she was saying was, she had found her perfect niche with you.

JACK.   Yeah well. If you've got a niche, scratch it. *(Small pause.)* Sorry.

DAWN.   What — ?

JACK.   Nothing.

DAWN.   If you've got a...?

PHYLLIS.   Just Jack being funny.

DAWN.   But what about *your* big deal?

JACK.   The what?

DAWN.   The deal out west. Did you close on it?

JACK.   Oh. Yeah, we closed on it.

DAWN.   So now you can pay off the house on the Vineyard and you'll be set for life.

JACK.   I guess.

PHYLLIS.   Are you okay?

DAWN.   Jack ...

JACK.   Huh?

DAWN.   *What happened?* You know? *(He stares at her.)*

JACK.   What did you say...?

DAWN.   Oh nothing. Just something stupid *Barry* picked up from his ex.

PHYLLIS.   You mean his *ex* ex.

DAWN.   Ruth. The dragon lady.

PHYLLIS.   I saw Barry the other day.

DAWN.   Oh yeah? What did he have to say for himself?

67

PHYLLIS. Not much.

DAWN. I'll bet. Does he have a job yet?

PHYLLIS. I don't think so. He asked me how you were.

DAWN. I hope you gave him hell.

PHYLLIS. I said that you were fine.

DAWN. Jerk ... *(Jack suddenly shifts as if he's about to rise.)*

PHYLLIS. Jack, what's the matter?

JACK. Nothing. Nothing. Just — nothing.

PHYLLIS. Do you want to go home?

JACK. No. Let's stay. Let's order something.

PHYLLIS. Are you sure?

JACK. Yeah. Let's chow down. Or chow up. Or chow in some direction ...

PHYLLIS. You don't have a headache, do you?

JACK. Nope. Nope nope nope nope ...

PHYLLIS. Scratch my neck. *(He lightly scratches the nape of her neck.)*

DAWN. Anybody know what "joyau de la chasse" is? I always forget to ask.

PHYLLIS. Joy of the chase?

JACK. Crown of the chase. Wild fowl stuffed with venison.

PHYLLIS. How did you know that?

JACK. I don't know. Doesn't everybody know that?

PHYLLIS. *I* didn't know that.

DAWN. I guess he must've had it with some other woman, Phil.

PHYLLIS. I guess so.

DAWN. That is a great wife you got there, you know.

JACK. I know.

DAWN. Don't you ever lose her, mister.

JACK. I wasn't planning on it.

DAWN. That girl is solid gold.

PHYLLIS. Maybe I'd better leave.

DAWN. Oh sit down. We're all adults here.

JACK. We are? *(Bell. Jack Exits. Another bell.)*

SCENE SIX

DAWN. I saw Jack today.

PHYLLIS. *(Reaching for a cigarette.)* Oh yeah...? How's he?

DAWN. Maybe you should give him a call.

PHYLLIS. I think I'm past Jack, thank you. Past Jack ... past Bob ... past Allen, past Manuel, past Fred, past Igor ...

DAWN. But are you past waiters? That one over there is kinda cute.

PHYLLIS. Oh come on.

DAWN. We could order up a little meatloaf.

PHYLLIS. I'm also past picking up strange waiters in restaurants.

DAWN. I don't know ... He doesn't look so strange to me.

PHYLLIS. Don't you *ever* give up?

DAWN. Nope.

PHYLLIS. You know — I don't honestly know what I'd do without you ... *(Bell. Dawn leaves. Bell.)*

SCENE SEVEN

PHYLLIS. Waiter! *(She smiles at him sweetly.)*

BLACKOUT

PROPERTY LIST

4 menus
4 sets of silverware wrapped in cloth napkins
4 water glasses
Sugar shaker
Ashtray
Book (RUTH)
Cigarettes and lighter (PHYLLIS)
Small vase, with rose
Hotel-desk bell, for off stage

A NOTE ABOUT THE SET:

In the original production, the restaurant booth was designed in four sections, each of them on hidden casters. At each character's exit, the person didn't need to rise and exit. Rather, a stagehand in the wings would pull that character's section of the booth away by hauling on a hidden rod. That character would be pulled off, the next character would take the empty seat, the unseen stagehand would push the booth section back into place, and the action would continue.

Short of that approach, a table with four chairs may be used.

MERE MORTALS

MERE MORTALS was presented at the Ensemble Studio Theatre (Curt Dempster, Artistic Director), in New York City, in June, 1990. It was directed by Jason McConnell Buzas; the set design was by Linda Giering Balmuth; the costume design was by Leslie McGovern, and the lighting design was by Greg MacPherson. The cast was as follows:

JOE .... Robert Pastorelli
CHARLIE .... Brian Smiar
FRANK.. Anthony LaPaglia

CHARACTERS

CHARLIE, FRANK and JOE, construction workers

JOE and FRANK are in their 30s.
CHARLIE is 55.

SETTING

A girder on the 50th floor of a new, unfinished skyscraper. One end of the girder is still unattached and hanging in open space.

MERE MORTALS

Joe is sitting astride the girder, near its attached end. He is unwrapping a sandwich he's taken from his lunch pail and is reading the newspaper with intense absorption. A bird sails by. Joe doesn't notice. A couple of small clouds sail by. Joe doesn't notice.

He looks up, thinking about something in the paper.

JOE.   Incredible. *(He goes back to the paper. Off, we hear Charlie singing something like "The Man Who Broke the Bank at Monte Carlo."* A moment later, he and Frank enter, both with lunch pails.)*

CHARLIE.   Hey Joe.

JOE.   Hey Charlie.

FRANK.   Hey Joe.

JOE.   Hey Frank. *(Charlie goes out to the very end of the girder and stands looking out. Frank sits midway on the girder and opens his lunch pail.)*

CHARLIE.   Think we're gonna make fifty today?

JOE.   *(Keeps reading.)* Looks like it.

CHARLIE.   Fifty stories down, fifty stories to go. I think we're gonna have this baby all punched in a week ahead of schedule.

JOE.   Yeah ...

CHARLIE.   Excelsior! *(Now he sits, on the very end, and opens his lunch pail.)* So. What's the bill of fare today? Frankie, what've you got?

FRANK.   *(Peering into his sandwich.)* I think it's liverwurst.

CHARLIE.   Joe? How 'bout you?

---

* See Special Note on Songs and Recordings on copyright page.

JOE. *(Reading.)* Pickle and pimento loaf.

FRANK. *(Looking into his sandwich again.)* Wait a minute. It's not liverwurst. It's tuna. I think. *(Sniffs it.)*

CHARLIE. Well *I* got corned beef and pastrami.

FRANK. Charlie, is that tuna, or liv — Corned *beef?*

CHARLIE. And Poupon mustard.

FRANK. On a normal Tuesday? What's the occasion?

CHARLIE. Who says there's an occasion?

FRANK. You hear that, Joe? Charlie's got corned beef and pastrami on a normal Tuesday.

CHARLIE. On bakery pumpernickel.

JOE. *(Not interested.)* Huh.

CHARLIE. Look at all those poor souls down there, have to eat their lunch at sea-level.

FRANK. *(Noting Joe's absorption in the paper.)* What's the news today, Joe? Something hot in the paper?

JOE. *(Doesn't look up.)* Hm?

FRANK. Some kinda ... international relations development? *(Joe looks up.)*

JOE. The news is that history is a cesspool.

FRANK. Oh.

JOE. As it always was. *(Goes back to the paper.)*

FRANK. Huh. *(Thinks about that for a moment.)* Well gimme the TV page, will you? Let's see what's on the tube.

CHARLIE. Don't let me hear nothing about TV.

FRANK. I just want to see —

CHARLIE. Don't let me hear no talk about TV. We got bowling tonight.

FRANK. I just want to see what I'm missing.

CHARLIE. Speaking of which, who's in for tonight?

FRANK. I'm in.

CHARLIE. Joe, are you in?

JOE. I can't this week, Charlie.

CHARLIE. You want to bowl a few games tonight?

JOE. I got things I got to do at home.

CHARLIE. What, you gotta nail up some doilies in your wife's powder room or something?

JOE. I got some things I got to do at —

CHARLIE. So do 'em tomorrow.

JOE. Bridget wants me to do 'em tonight.

CHARLIE. So bring her along and do 'em tomorrow.

JOE. I can't do 'em tomorrow, I —

CHARLIE. Hey who's the king in your house, anyway? Who is the king? Who makes the rules?

FRANK. Gentlemen ...

JOE. When Maggie wanted you to put in that new floor, you didn't bowl for two weeks, Charlie.

CHARLIE. That was different.

JOE. And because you couldn't bowl, you wouldn't let *us* bowl neither.

CHARLIE. That was different.

JOE. Yeah why was it so different?

CHARLIE. Just don't get small on me, Joe, okay?

JOE. Why was it so —

CHARLIE. I hate it when you get *small* on me like that.

FRANK. Gentlemen, *please!* (*Joe and Charlie are quiet. After a moment.*)

JOE. And it's not doilies.

FRANK. Joe. (*Joe is quiet.*) How 'bout that lawn mower you bought, Charlie? How's that working?

CHARLIE. Aaaaah, it's busted.

FRANK. No.

CHARLIE. Yeah, it's ...

FRANK. Already?

CHARLIE. Yeah.

FRANK. So did you take it back?

CHARLIE. Aah, I don't know why I ever cut my grass in the first place. I *like* it long. I like to sit on my porch and look at it long. Where do you think the word "lawn" comes from in the first place? From "long," because grass was always *long.* Originally people said I'm gonna plant some seeds and grow a long. Then some moron thought he'd be different and cut his long short. The rest is the history of fashion.

FRANK. I didn't know that. (*Joe snickers.*)

CHARLIE. You say something, Joe?

JOE. Who, me? No, I didn't say nothing. *(A paper floats by. Charlie plucks it effortlessly out of the air, glances at it cursorily, lets it float away again.)*

FRANK. *(Looks up and calls.)* Hep Peptak! You got any of them sugar cubes? *(He holds out the cup of his thermos and a sugar cube drops into it from above.)* Thanks! *(An air mattress floats by. No reaction from any of them.)*

CHARLIE. You guys ever think about hang-gliding home from here?

FRANK. Hang-gliding home?

CHARLIE. Yeah, instead of driving or taking the Path? *(Frank thinks about that a moment.)*

FRANK. Wouldn't you have to learn how to hang-glide first?

CHARLIE. Well sure, you'd learn. But then after you wrapped up work you could just strap on your wings — walk off the top floor — and sail home. Be the first person in history to fly from 13th Street and Twelfth Avenue to Tenafly, New Jersey. With a fabulous view all the way. *(Small pause.)* Maybe after I retire.

FRANK. You know I been sitting here eating this thing and I still don't know if it's tuna or liverwurst?

CHARLIE. Yeah well that's all the ozone up here.

FRANK. The what?

CHARLIE. All the carbon dioxide up here compresses the things in your nose, and you can't taste nothing. *(Joe snickers, louder than before.)* Did you say something, Joe?

JOE. Not me. I guess the carbon dioxide was compressing my nose or something.

FRANK. *(Glancing at the newspaper.)* Speaking of flying, Charlie, they got that movie about the Lindbergh kid on again tonight.

CHARLIE. They got the what?

FRANK. That show about the Lindbergh baby who got kidnapped, with —

CHARLIE. Let me see that. *(He grabs the paper from Frank's hand.)*

FRANK. Hey, what's up? What the hell you doing?

CHARLIE. I just want to see. *(Reads intently.)*

FRANK. Did you see that movie that time it was on?

CHARLIE. Yeah ...

FRANK. Anthony Hopkins, as what's-his-name ...

CHARLIE. Bruno Hauptmann.

FRANK. Hey didn't that happen someplace around — ?

CHARLIE. Hopewell, New Jersey.

JOE. What are they bringing that turkey back for?

CHARLIE. "Turkey?"

JOE. Yeah, who wants to see that garbage all over again?

CHARLIE. It happens to be a very thoughtful movie, for your information. And as it happens they show that movie every year on the anniversary of the day that Charles Lindbergh's baby was kidnapped.

JOE. That happened 50 years ago! What's the big deal about —

CHARLIE. Jesus Christ died on Easter, they show "The King of Kings" that weekend.

FRANK. Gentlemen ...

CHARLIE. If you'd ever done anything more important than glue your wife's cat pictures into a photo album, they'd show the "Joe Morelli Story" on *your* birthday. Does that explain to you why the movie is on today?

FRANK. Gentlemen, please!

CHARLIE. And don't let me hear the word "turkey."

FRANK. Hey what's with you today, Charlie? What's the matter?

CHARLIE. Nothing's the matter.

FRANK. You're acting all weird.

CHARLIE. I'm not weird.

FRANK. So what's up?

JOE. Turkey.

CHARLIE. I TOLD YOU I DON'T WANT TO HEAR THE WORD "TURKEY!"

FRANK. Something sure seems up.

CHARLIE. Nothing is up. Forget about it. Nothing's up. *(Brief pause.)*

FRANK. Here, bird. *(He whistles to a passing bird, and tosses it a crumb. Charlie has taken a cupcake out of his lunch pail, try-*

ing to keep it out of sight of the others. The cupcake has a candle stuck in it.) What the heck is *that?*

CHARLIE.   What does it look like? It's a cupcake.

FRANK.   Hey Joe, will you look at this?

JOE.   Isn't that nice. Maggie made him a cupcake.

CHARLIE.   My wife did *not* make me this cupcake, I *bought* this cupcake.

FRANK.   What's the celebration, Charlie?

CHARLIE.   Who says there's a celebration?

FRANK.   Corned beef and pastrami and now a chocolate cupcake?

CHARLIE.   *(Pointing to the cupcake.)* A somber color, if you will notice. Maybe I'm, maybe I'm observing a very solemn day for some private reason.

JOE.   Next thing you know he's going to be putting out doilies around his house.

CHARLIE.   That's it, Morelli!

FRANK.   Gentlemen —

JOE.   And your taste in movies is lousy —

FRANK.   Gentlemen —

JOE.   And if you ask me, Charles Lindbergh is overrated.

CHARLIE.   Overrated?

JOE.   Yeah, overrated! So he flew across the —

CHARLIE.   The greatest hero in American history?

JOE.   He flew across the ocean. *Big deal.*

CHARLIE.   Oh big deal, huh?

JOE.   Yeah. And as for the Lindbergh baby — who *cares?*

CHARLIE.   Who cares?

JOE.   Who the hell cares, it's old news!

CHARLIE.   Oh yeah?

JOE.   It's fifty years ago that kid got stolen.

CHARLIE.   Well for your inform —

JOE.   Working people get kidnapped every day in the world and they don't make no movies about *them.*

CHARLIE.   Maybe they're not as import —

JOE.   In Argentina, in Russia, in Indonesia —

FRANK.   Now let's not insult our Russian brothers —

JOE.   So why am I supposed to care about the goddamn

Lindbergh baby?

CHARLIE.   You don't care about the Lindbergh baby?

JOE.   No, I don't care about the Lindbergh baby.

CHARLIE.   You don't have any feeling for the Lindbergh baby?

JOE.   No I don't have any feeling for the —

CHARLIE.   Well for your information, *I am the Lindbergh baby.* *(Pause.)*

FRANK.   You're the...?

CHARLIE.   *Yes.* I am the Lindbergh baby. I am the rightful son of Charles Lindbergh, kidnapped from the home of my parents, and I didn't mean to tell you but you forced me into it. And the hell if I will listen to my family being insulted! So there! *(Pause.)*

JOE.   You're the — ?

CHARLIE.   Yes.

FRANK.   But your name is Petrossian.

CHARLIE.   Oh sure. That's what I was brought up to *think* my name was.

JOE.   YOU THINK YOU'RE THE LINDBERGH BABY?

CHARLIE.   Go to hell, Joe.

JOE.   Have you gone off your head?

CHARLIE.   No I have not gone off my head.

JOE.   I don't believe this!

CHARLIE.   Yeah well the truth is always strange at first sight. So live with it.

JOE.   Do you know that there are separate asylums to hold all the people who think they're the Lindbergh baby?

CHARLIE.   Just mind your own business, will you? Read your newspaper. Stick to pickle and pimento loaf, Smalltime.

FRANK.   Charlie, there *are* people who might wonder a little, if you claimed to be the Lindbergh baby.

CHARLIE.   But it all fits, doesn't it? I mean — "Charles?" "Charlie?" Was I not born in New Jersey? Was I not brought up in the town of Hopewell, where the crime was perpetrated? *(Frank thinks a moment.)*

FRANK.   He *was* brought up in Hopewell, Joe.

JOE.   Yeah? That makes about 50,000 other Lindbergh babies.

CHARLIE.   Well they're impostors.

FRANK.   I thought the police found the kid's body.

CHARLIE.   That was another kid's body.

FRANK.   Whose body?

CHARLIE.   I don't know whose body. But it wasn't *my* body.

FRANK.   Obviously not.... How come you kept this a secret all these years, Charlie?

JOE.   Because people would think he was a fruitcake, that's why.

CHARLIE.   I am talking to Frank!

JOE.   Okay. Okay.

FRANK.   So how come you kept it secret.

CHARLIE.   Well naturally a lot of people probably wouldn't believe me.

JOE.   OH REALLY?

CHARLIE.   Plus I was already pretty well established as Charles Petrossian. You know — driver's license, credit cards, bank account ...

FRANK.   Sure, sure, it's hard to make a change.

CHARLIE.   But mostly I didn't want to upset the feelings of my true mother, Anne Morrow Lindbergh.

JOE.   Whose books are bullshit.

CHARLIE.   You shut your trap about my mother!

FRANK.   Come on, Joe, you know better than that.

JOE.   Have you read her books?

CHARLIE.   Yes I have and I think they're very beautiful.

JOE.   She made a goddamn fortune off of you, writing about that kidnapping.

CHARLIE.   It happened to be a very traumatic experience for her.

JOE.   That don't mean she has to go peddle it on the street corner. You oughta ask for a cut of her royalties. You could retire early, take up *hang-gliding.*

CHARLIE.   I'm through talking to you.

FRANK.   Joe's got a good point, Charlie. You ought to contact the family. You could try to pick up your inheritance. You coulda been a rich guy, Charlie!

CHARLIE. Actually ... I did try to write to mother, once.
FRANK. You did?
CHARLIE. Yeah. But she never answered back. I figure the letter never got to her.
FRANK. Did you tell her — you know — who you were?
CHARLIE. I *hinted* who I was.
JOE. Oh sure. "Dear Mom." And then he signed it, "Your loving son, Charles Petrossian." "P.S. — please send the inheritance."
CHARLIE. Knock it off.
JOE. Real subtle.
CHARLIE. Anyway I told her how I was from her area. That's how I put it, I said that I was "from her *area.*"
FRANK. That's a hint.
JOE. Sigmund Freud would've had a picnic.
CHARLIE. I told her how I saw their house lots of times.
FRANK. You saw the house you were kidnapped from?
CHARLIE. Sure. I used to go by it all the time when I was a kid. Then later on when I knew who I really was I used to drive out there sometimes and just park and look at it. I'd park under this tree and sit there thinking to myself, This is yours, Charlie. This is your kingdom.
FRANK. So your old man flew the Atlantic in the Spirit of St. Louis.
CHARLIE. And my grandfather was Ambassador to Mexico.
FRANK. I didn't know that.
CHARLIE. Yeah, my mother's father.
FRANK. I seen the movie lots of times on the late show, "The Spirit of St. Louis." Must be great, having Jimmy Stewart play your father and all.
CHARLIE. I wrote to Jimmy once, under my nom de plume of Petrossian.
FRANK. He ever answer back?
CHARLIE. I got a signed picture in the mail.
FRANK. You never told me that!
CHARLIE. Yeah.
FRANK. You never told me you had a signed picture of Jimmy Stewart!

CHARLIE. Well I been keeping it a secret in case people start getting ideas about my true identity. Somebody puts a few clues together, it could have repercussions.

JOE. Yeah, they'd throw you in the loony bin.

CHARLIE. Go ahead. Scoff if you will!

FRANK. But this means Anthony Hopkins didn't really do it.

CHARLIE. You mean kidnap me?

FRANK. Yeah.

CHARLIE. Obviously not. Not unless he was in league with the Petrossian family, and handed me over to them.

FRANK. Yeah — what *about* the Petrossians' role in all this?

CHARLIE. My foster parents, as I like to think of them? Pawns in a bigger game, Frank. Pawns in a bigger game.

FRANK. Yeah. But how did you make the transition? I mean, from being a Lindbergh to being a Petrossian?

CHARLIE. Let me just say, I got my ideas, Frankie.

FRANK. You know it's very funny you should be saying all this.

CHARLIE. What, that I've been the Lindbergh baby all these years and you never knew it?

FRANK. Yeah. Because you see, I'm the son of Czar Nicholas the Second of Russia.

CHARLIE. No.

FRANK. Yeah.

CHARLIE. You're kidding.

FRANK. It's the truth.

CHARLIE. The kid that got killed in the Russian Revolution?

FRANK. That's me. The heir to the throne of Moscow.

CHARLIE. Holy shit.

FRANK. And Sovereign of the Ukraine.

CHARLIE. I saw that movie. "Nicholas and What's-Her-Name."

FRANK. Alexandra. That was *my* mother.

CHARLIE. But I thought you got shot.

FRANK. A faithful servant smuggled me out. Nobody knows I survived.

CHARLIE. And you had Laurence Olivier in your movie and everything. I mean, Anthony Hopkins is one thing — but Sir Laurence Olivier! That's hot stuff!

FRANK. Yeah, I felt pretty honored, having him in my movie. Though I did have a few quibbles about the, you know, historical details.

CHARLIE. So then what's your real name?

FRANK. Alexei Nikolaievitch Romanoff.

CHARLIE. By what name would you prefer to be called? *(Frank considers that. Then.)*

FRANK. Why don't you just keep calling me Frank. It'll be easier.

CHARLIE. Besides protecting your incognito.

JOE. THE CZAR OF RUSSIA?

CHARLIE. Now Joe —

JOE. THE CZAR OF *RUSSIA?*

CHARLIE. I don't want to hear a word from you, Joe.

JOE. Do you know how old you'd have to be, to be the Czar of Russia?

CHARLIE. Never you mind, Frank.

JOE. You'd have to be 90 years old!

CHARLIE. You want to hurt his feelings?

JOE. And a hemophiliac!

FRANK. I've always been a heavy bleeder.

JOE. That don't make you the goddamn Czar of Russia! I mean, the Lindbergh baby is one thing, but —

CHARLIE. Will you just shut up? Please? Shut up? You're on a lot of very sensitive ground. We are talking families, Joe. And Frank here lost everybody in the Revolution, so have a little sympathy. You got orphans here.

JOE. Okay then, Alexei. How do you know all this? How do you know you're the head honcho of the Ukraine?

FRANK. Well ... one day I saw this picture in a book, a picture of Moscow with the ... you know ... the Kremlin, and those domes —

CHARLIE. Yeah, those onion-shaped domes.

FRANK. And I said to myself, I've been there! I've been

there sometime! It was like I could remember it.

CHARLIE. Of course you'd remember it. Those communist bastards tried to rub you out there.

FRANK. And then when I saw that movie it was like I knew all the streets. Before they'd even go around a corner I'd know what was going to be on the other side. It was home.

CHARLIE. Musta been painful.

FRANK. It was pretty painful.

CHARLIE. Seeing everything you lost out on.

FRANK. It only got really bad when I had to watch myself get killed.

CHARLIE. Understandably, Alexei. Understandably. But how's your Russian these days?

FRANK. Oh, I've forgotten most of it by now.

CHARLIE. The whole trauma probably made you — you know —

FRANK. Repress it.

CHARLIE. Plus the strain of having to maintain your daily identity as Frank Mikula. Have you told Phyllis?

FRANK. No, she doesn't know. I'll probably have to tell her sometime, though.

CHARLIE. I think she'll understand.

FRANK. I just have to wait for the right — you know —

CHARLIE. Circumstances.

FRANK. Circumstances.

CHARLIE. She'd probably be pretty surprised to find out she's the Queen of Russia.

FRANK. Czarina.

CHARLIE. Huh?

FRANK. The wife of the Czar in the Czarina.

CHARLIE. Is that proof, Joe? I say queen, he says czarina. He's got the facts at the tips of his fingers.

JOE. I know how cars work, but that don't make me an Oldsmobile.

FRANK. Peace, gentlemen.

CHARLIE. Okay.

FRANK. Peace.

CHARLIE.   Just think, if we had you over there running things instead of those red bastards, we could all sleep a little better at night.

FRANK.   I know. That's the hardest thing about being — you know —

CHARLIE.   Who you are.

FRANK.   Who I am. Knowing what I could do for world peace if everybody knew who I really am.

CHARLIE.   Well if things had worked out different, I can't think of anybody I'd rather have on the Russian throne than you, Frank.

FRANK.   Thanks, Charlie.

CHARLIE.   Yeah ... Well I'll be goddamned. To think all this time we never knew it. You didn't know about me, and I didn't know about you. And Joe didn't know about either one of us ... *(Silence. They turn and look at Joe.)*

FRANK.   So, Joe.

JOE.   Yeah, what?

FRANK.   Who are *you?*

JOE.   I'm not anybody.

FRANK.   Really, I mean.

JOE.   I'm not anybody.

FRANK.   *Really.*

JOE.   I'm Joe Morelli. Period.

FRANK.   I'm not talking about that.

JOE.   I'm Superman.

FRANK.   I mean really.

JOE.   I'm nobody.

FRANK.   Underneath it all.

JOE.   I'm nobody. I'm just another guy on the street. *(Pause.)* But I *was* Marie Antoinette in a previous life.

CHARLIE.   No shit!

JOE.   Yeah, that was me!

FRANK.   The let-'em-eat-cake lady?

JOE.   I said that in 1793.

CHARLIE.   Isn't that something.

FRANK.   I knew you were *some*body.

CHARLIE. Frank gets shot up by the Reds and you have your head chopped off in Paris.

JOE. Yeah. One minute I'm Marie Antoinette standing on the scaffold, the next minute I'm Joe Morelli in Weehawken.

CHARLIE. Must be pretty disconcerting.

JOE. To say the least. But I do remember the — *(Bell rings off.)*

CHARLIE. Aaah shit.

FRANK. Already?

JOE. It's one o'clock?

CHARLIE. That's what the company says.

JOE. Jesus. *(They start to pack up their things.)* But listen, you guys — you can't tell anybody.

FRANK. You forget who you're talking to.

JOE. I don't want this getting around.

FRANK. We know that, Joe.

JOE. People would think I was kinda weird.

CHARLIE. We will be as the tomb.

JOE. You swear?

CHARLIE. Of course we swear.

FRANK. We're all in the same — you know —

CHARLIE. Situation.

FRANK. Situation.

CHARLIE. But now first things first. Who is bowling tonight?

FRANK. I'm in.

CHARLIE. And I'm in. Joey?

JOE. I told you, Charlie. I got all these things to do.

CHARLIE. You gonna let that bullshit get in your way? Are you forgetting who you are?

FRANK. Yeah, Joe. *Remember the crown jewels.*

JOE. You're right. Count me in.

CHARLIE. Great.

JOE. And c'est la guerre.

FRANK. But you know, Charlie, if you want to stay home and watch the Lindbergh movie tonight — we'll understand completely.

CHARLIE. Naah, I've seen it. Let's bowl.

FRANK. Okay. *(They start out along the girder.)*
JOE. Long as I'm home by midnight.
CHARLIE. What are you — Cinderella? *(They exit along the girder, Charlie singing. A bird sails by.)*

LIGHTS FADE

PROPERTY LIST

3 lunch pails
3 wrapped sandwiches
3 thermoses
3 hardhats
Newspaper (JOE)
Sugar cube, for Frank
An air mattress
Cupcake, with candle in it (CHARLIE)
A bird
A couple of small clouds
A piece of paper

SPEED-THE-PLAY

this is for Martha Stoberock
with love
because it made her laugh
and just because

SPEED-THE-PLAY was performed at the Mitzi Newhouse Theater of Lincoln Center on November 20, 1989, as part of a benefit for Broadway Cares hosted by *Spy* Magazine and honoring David Mamet. The evening was directed by Gregory Mosher, and the cast was as follows:

American Buffalo

DONNY	J.J. Johnston
BOBBY	W.H. Macy
TEACH	Mike Nussbaum

Speed-the-Plow

GOULD	Joe Mantegna
FOX	Bob Balaban
KAREN	Felicity Huffman

Sexual Perversity in Chicago

BERNIE	Treat Williams
DANNY	Steven Goldstein
DEBORAH	Mariel Hemingway
JOAN	Felicity Huffman

Glengarry Glen Ross

LEVENE	Robert Prosky
WILLIAMSON	W.H. Macy
MOSS	J.J. Johnston
AARONOW	Mike Nussbaum
ROMA	Joe Mantegna
CUSTOMER	Steven Goldstein

M.C.   Roderick McLachlan

THE SETTING

A podium, for the M.C. Otherwise, as little as possible, gotten on and off as quickly as possible:

American Buffalo: a table and two chairs, and a pigsticker on the table (looks like a crowbar).

Speed-the-Plow: a desk with a couple of chairs for the office at left, and a couple of chairs at right for the couch.

Sexual Perversity in Chicago: two chairs and a cafe table at left, a file cabinet upstage center for the office, and a small bed at right for the bedroom scenes.

Glengarry Glen Ross: two chairs, center, for the restaurant scenes.

SPEED-THE-PLAY

The M.C. enters, at a podium.

M.C.   David Mamet. Poker player. Cigar smoker. Male bonder. Winner of the Pulitzer Prize. Film director. Chicagoan. *Genius.* Why is David Mamet a genius? Because from a very early age, he instinctively knew three important things about his audience. First — Americans like speed. Things that are fast. This is, after all, the country that invented the rock song and the roller coaster, and might have invented premature ejaculation if it hadn't been invented already. So Mamet keeps his plays in fifth gear. Second — David Mamet knows that Americans don't like to pay for parking. So he keeps his plays short. Third — he knows how Americans talk. Particularly American men. He appreciates that when American men go to the theatre, they want to hear familiar words like "asshole," and "jagoff." Which might explain the popularity of *American Buffalo,* in which the word "fuck" appears over 16,000 times. We are gathered here tonight to honor David Mamet for his contribution to the American theatre. Some of you might not be familiar with the Master's work, so we have, as it were, boiled down a few of the major plays and extracted the gist, to give you the Master's *oovruh* in the Master's own way: short, and to the fuckin' *point.* Four plays in seven minutes. You are about to enter ... the Mamet Zone. *(He rings a fight bell.) American Buffalo.* Act One. A junkshop. *(Donny and Bobby enter.)*

DONNY.   Bobby, you're a young punk.

BOBBY.   Fuckin' right I am.

DONNY.   A small-time thief.

BOBBY.   Fuckin' right I am.

DONNY.   But we never use the word "thief" do we, Bobby?

BOBBY.   Fuckin' right we don't.

95

DONNY.   And do you fence stolen goods through my junk shop?

BOBBY.   We never talk about it.

DONNY.   Fuckin' right we don't.

BOBBY.   So what do we talk about, Donny?

DONNY.   The nature of life. We also say "fuck" a lot. *(Teach enters.)*

TEACH.   Fuckin' life.

DONNY.   Is it bad, Teach?

TEACH.   It's very bad.

DONNY.   Go for more coffee, Bob. *(Bobby exits.)*

TEACH.   Fuckin' Fletcher. Fuckin' Ruthie.

DONNY.   You ran into Ruthie heretofore?

TEACH.   I'm over in the coffee shop puttin' my finger on the Zeitgeist, Ruthie's sittin' there talkin' objective correlatives. Bull*shit*, I say. Next thing I know, form follows content, this fuckin' cunt is traveling around the corner with my sweetroll! For which I paid for, sixty-fi' cents plus a truckload of stolen pig-iron. Now is that the mirror back to nature, or what? As for fuckin' I-don't-*give*-a-shit-what-anybody-says *Fletcher,* I say the guy is a hairdresser, and I only hope some vicious lesbo with a zipgun rips his fuckin' lips off, sends 'em in to *Boys' Life* magazine, and prints 'em in a two-page spread that says Oh, *Shit* to all eternity. *(Pause.)* What's new?

DONNY.   Not much. I was thinkin' I'd ask Bobby to steal some rare coins for me tonight.

TEACH.   Maybe I should do it instead.

DONNY.   Okay. *(Bell.)*

M.C.   Act Two. The junkshop, that night. *(Teach and Donny enter.)*

TEACH.   Everything's fucked up, Donny. I can't steal the rare coins.

DONNY.   I fear I detect a rationalization, Teach.

TEACH.   Why don't you go take a leak in the gene pool you swam in on. *(Bobby enters.)*

BOBBY.   Hey, Don. Want to buy this rare buffalo-head nickel?

TEACH.   Fuck you, Bobby. *(He hits Bobby with a pig-sticker.)*

96

BOBBY.   OW!

DONNY.   Fuck you, Teach.

TEACH.   Fuck you, Donny.

BOBBY.   Fuck you, Donny and Teach. *(Pause.)*

TEACH.   So is there anything more to say? *(Three bells.)*

M.C.   *Speed The Plough.* Act One. An office in Hollywood. *(A bell rings. Fox and Gould enter.)*

FOX.   Gould, you are the new head of production at this studio.

GOULD.   I am.

FOX.   I am an unsuccessful independent producer.

GOULD.   You are.

FOX.   And you owe me a favor.

GOULD.   Forsooth?

FOX.   I own this piece-a-shit movie script. Will you take it to the head of the studio and make me rich?

GOULD.   I'll do it at ten o'clock tomorrow morning.

FOX.   Thank you, Gould.

GOULD.   I'm a whore.

FOX.   I'm a whore too.

GOULD.   And we're *men.*

FOX.   Who's your sexy new secretary?

GOULD.   Some fuckin' temp.

FOX.   I bet you 500 bills you can't get her in the sack.

GOULD.   It's a bet. *(Into intercom.)* Karen, would you come in here, please? (Karen enters.)

KAREN.   Sir?

GOULD.   Karen, would you read this book about cosmic bullshit that somebody submitted and come to my house tonight to report on it?

KAREN.   Yes sir. *(She exits.)*

GOULD.   Consider her fucked. *(Bell.)*

M.C.   Act Two. Gould's house, that evening. *(Gould and Karen are in the house area.)*

GOULD.   Did you read the book about cosmic bullshit, Karen?

KAREN.   Yes and I think the book is brilliant.

GOULD.   It might be.

KAREN. And Mr. Fox's script is trash.

GOULD. It may be.

KAREN. So why will you produce it?

GOULD. Because I'm a whore.

KAREN. *I* think you're a very sensitive man.

GOULD. At last a girl who understands me! *(They embrace. Bell.)*

M.C. Act Three. Gould's office, the next morning. *(Gould and Fox enter.)*

GOULD. I'm not gonna recommend your script, Fox.

FOX. No?

GOULD. I'm not going to the head of the studio with it.

FOX. No?

GOULD. I'm gonna recommend this brilliant book on cosmic bullshit instead. Why? Because the business of America ... is Byzantine.

FOX. You lift your leg to pee.

GOULD. You genuflect to pick your nose.

FOX. You stand on your head to jerk off.

GOULD. You bounce on a trampoline to defecate.

FOX. You know you're only doing this because that shtupka went to bed with you. Fired off a 21-gun salute on your weenie. *(Small pause.)*

GOULD. You're right. *(Into intercom.)* Karen, would you come in here, please? *(Karen enters.)*

KAREN. Bob ... Bob ... Bob ...

GOULD. You're fired. *(Karen exits.)*

FOX. She's a whore.

GOULD. She's a whore.

FOX. And you're my friend.

GOULD. If only we were women, we could be lesbians together.

FOX. But in the meantime, life —

GOULD. — is very good. *(Three bells.)*

M.C. *Sexual Perversity in Chicago.* Scene One. A singles bar. *(Bell. Donny and Bernie enter.)*

BERNIE. All women are alike, Donny.

DONNY. Gosh, Bernie. Is that really true?

BERNIE. Essentially they're bitches.

DONNY. Or else they're whores?

BERNIE. Yes. Or else they're whores. *(Bell.)*

M.C. Scene Two. Joan and Deborah's apartment. *(Joan and Deborah enter.)*

JOAN. All men are alike, Deborah.

DEBORAH. They certainly are, Joan.

JOAN and DEBORAH. They're *men. (Bell.)*

M.C. Scene Three. A singles bar. *(Joan, alone. Bernie enters.)*

BERNIE. Hi there.

JOAN. Get lost.

BERNIE. You got a lotta fuckin' nerve. *(Bell.)*

M.C. Scene Four. A library. *(Deborah, alone. Donny enters.)*

DONNY. Hi there.

DEBORAH. Get lost.

DONNY. Want to go out with me?

DEBORAH. Okay. *(Bell.)*

M.C. Scene Five. Bernie's apartment. *(Bernie, alone.)*

BERNIE. Is there a metaphysical point to broads? *(Bell.)*

M.C. Scene Six. Donny's apartment. *(Donny and Deborah in bed.)*

DONNY. Nice nice, Deborah.

DEBORAH. Nice nice, Donny.

DONNY and DEBORAH. Goodnight! *(They fall asleep. Bell.)*

M.C. Scene Seven. A bar. *(Donny, Deborah and Bernie.)*

DONNY. *(Introducing.)* Bernie, Deborah. Deborah, Bernie.

DEBORAH and BERNIE. Hello!

BERNIE. You sure are a nice girl, Deborah. *(Aside to Donny.)* Probably a whore. *(Bell.)*

M.C. Scene Eight. Donny and Bernie's office.

BERNIE. Donny, people sometimes have sexual intercourse under very peculiar circumstances.

DONNY. Is that true, Bernie?

BERNIE. Yes it is. *(Bell.)*

M.C. Scene Nine. Deborah and Joan's apartment. *(Joan and Deborah enter.)*

JOAN. Is there a metaphysical point to men? *(Deborah does not answer. Bell.)*

M.C.   Scene Ten. An office.

BERNIE.   Don't fall in love, Donny.

DONNY.   Mn.

BERNIE.   Deborah's just another bitch.

DONNY.   Mmn.

BERNIE.   I gather that you don't agree? *(Bell.)*

M.C.   Scene Eleven. Donny's apartment. *(Donny and Deborah in bed.)*

DONNY.   Breast.

DEBORAH.   Sperm.

DONNY.   Penis.

DEBORAH.   Menstruation.

DONNY.   Masturbation.

DEBORAH.   Your come smells just like Clorox. *(Pause.)*

DONNY.   I think I'm falling in love with you.

M.C.   He does so. *(Bell.)* Scene Twelve. A toy shop. *(Donny and Bernie enter.)*

BERNIE.   When I was a child, an old man once placed his hand on my genitals in a movie theatre.

DONNY.   On your genitals?

BERNIE.   In a movie theatre.

DONNY.   Was it psychologically damaging?

BERNIE.   How do I know, Donny? I was only a fucking child! *(Bell.)*

M.C.   Scene Thirteen. A restaurant. *(Deborah and Joan enter.)*

DEBORAH.   I'm going to move in with Donny. *(Joan puts a finger down her throat and gags. Bell.)*

M.C.   Scene Fourteen. The office. *(Bernie and Donny.)*

BERNIE.   Ba deep ba dop ba *doop*, Don.

DONNY.   I know that, Bernie.

BERNIE.   Da-da-daaa some girl, da-da-daaa it's love, da-da-daaa you're fucked. Oop scoop a wee-bop, bonk, *deek*!

DONNY.   Sure, I see your point. *(Bell.)*

M.C.   Scene Fifteen. Donny and Deborah's apartment. *(Donny and Deborah enter.)*

DONNY.   Where's the shampoo?

DEBORAH.   Will you still love me when I'm old?

DONNY.   Why are you putting on dirty pantyhose?

DEBORAH. Are we all right?

DONNY. Bitch.

DEBORAH. Jerk. I'm moving out. *(Bell.)*

M.C. Scene Sixteen. Deborah and Joan's apartment. *(Deborah and Joan enter.)*

JOAN. All men are alike, Deborah.

DEBORAH. Oh be quiet. *(Bell.)*

M.C. Scene Seventeen. A beach. *(Donny and Bernie enter, ogling women.)*

DONNY. All women are alike, Bernie.

BERNIE. Yes, they are.

DONNY. They're bitches.

BERNIE. Or else they're whores. And life, Donny boy?

DONNY. Life is good, Bernie.

BERNIE. Yes, life is *very* good. *(A bell rings three times.)*

M.C. *Glengarry Glen Ross.* Act one, scene one. A booth in a Chinese restaurant. *(Levene and Williamson in a booth.)*

LEVENE. John. John. John. Forty fifty sixty years I been the best goddamn hustler of swampland in the whole history of real estate scams. I started selling real estate before I was *born. I* hit the calls. *I* caught the marks. *I* platted out the stats. I ate the chalk. I made the fuckin' *board,* John.

WILLIAMSON. Uh-huh.

LEVENE. Now I wanna win that Cadillac as top salesman of the month, I need some leads.

WILLIAMSON. You can't have any leads, Shelley.

LEVENE. Oh *please,* John, *please? (Bell.)*

M.C. Scene Two. Another booth at the restaurant. *(Moss and Aaronow.)*

MOSS. We're gonna win that fuckin' Cadillac, Aaronow.

AARONOW. *Duhhh.*

MOSS. You and me. Know how?

AARONOW. *Duhhh.*

MOSS. We're gonna steal the leads from the office.

AARONOW. *Duhhh.*

MOSS. I mean you and me, Aaronow. Tonight. *(Aaronow thinks.)*

AARONOW. Wouldn't that be illegal? *(Bell.)*

M.C.   Scene Three. Another booth at the restaurant. *(Roma and a Potential Customer.)*

ROMA.   What is the meaning of life?

POTENTIAL CUSTOMER.   I don't know.

ROMA.   Me either. Would you like to buy some real estate? *(Bell.)*

M.C.   Act Two. The real estate office, the next morning. *(Williamson, Moss, Aaronow and Roma with a Policeman.)*

WILLIAMSON.   Somebody broke into the office last night and stole the leads. Was it you, Moss?

MOSS.   I ain't talkin'.

WILLIAMSON.   Was it you, Roma?

ROMA.   Suck my dick.

WILLIAMSON.   Was it you, Aaronow?

AARONOW.   *Duhhh. (Levene enters.)*

LEVENE.   *(Waving a paper.)* Hand over the Cadillac! I just made a sale!

WILLIAMSON.   Sorry, Levene. *You* were the one who stole the leads last night. *(To Policeman.)* Take Levene away.

LEVENE.   You can't take me away! I got the marks! I made the calls! I hit the board! I won the car! You can't do this to me!

WILLIAMSON.   Yes I can. We're illustrating the nature of American capitalism.

LEVENE.   Oh. Okay. *(Policeman takes him away.)*

AARONOW.   Can I have a Cadillac?

WILLIAMSON.   No.

ROMA.   Is there anybody here who hasn't said "fuck"? *(Small pause. Everybody shakes their head.)* I'll be at the restaurant.

BLACKOUT

PROPERTY LIST

Fight bell (M.C.)
Pig sticker (TEACH)

NEW
PLAYS

THE AFRICAN COMPANY PRESENTS
RICHARD III
by Carlyle Brown

EDWARD ALBEE'S
FRAGMENTS and THE MARRIAGE PLAY

IMAGINARY LIFE
by Peter Parnell

MIXED EMOTIONS
by Richard Baer

THE SWAN
by Elizabeth Egloff

Write for information as to
availability
DRAMATISTS PLAY SERVICE, Inc.
440 Park Avenue South   New York, N.Y. 10016

NEW
PLAYS

THE LIGHTS
by Howard Korder

THE TRIUMPH OF LOVE
by James Magruder

LATER LIFE
by A.R. Gurney

THE LOMAN FAMILY PICNIC
by Donald Margulies

A PERFECT GANESH
by Terrence McNally

SPAIN
by Romulus Linney

*Write for information as to
availability*
DRAMATISTS PLAY SERVICE, Inc.
440 Park Avenue South   New York, N.Y. 10016

NEW
PLAYS

LONELY PLANET
by Steven Dietz

THE AMERICA PLAY
by Suzan-Lori Parks

THE FOURTH WALL
by A.R. Gurney

JULIE JOHNSON
by Wendy Hammond

FOUR DOGS AND A BONE
by John Patrick Shanley

DESDEMONA, A PLAY ABOUT A
HANDKERCHIEF
by Paula Vogel

Write for information as to
availability
DRAMATISTS PLAY SERVICE, Inc.
440 Park Avenue South   New York, N.Y. 10016